ERASED

God's Complete Forgiveness of Sins

Gary L. Holmes

FIRE MOUNTAIN
PUBLISHING

We want to hear from you. Please send your comments about this book to us in care of gary@firemountainpublishing.com. Thank you.

ERASED: God's Complete Forgiveness of Sins
First Edition, August 2019

Copyright © 2019 Gary L. Holmes

Printed in the United States of America

All rights reserved. No part of this publication may be reproduced, distributed, or transmitted in any form or by any means, including photocopying, recording, or other electronic or mechanical methods, without the prior written permission of the publisher, except in the case of brief quotations embodied in critical reviews and certain other noncommercial uses permitted by copyright law.

ISBN: 978-1-64633-788-0 (hardcover)

ISBN: 978-0-57854-899-9 (paperback)

ISBN: 978-1-64633-787-3 (eBook)

Library of Congress Control Number: 2019910455

Publisher's Cataloging-in-Publication Data

Name: Holmes, Gary L., author.
Title: Erased: God's complete forgiveness of sins / Gary L. Holmes.
Description: Includes index | First edition | Mansfield, TX: Fire Mountain Publishing, 2019.
Identifiers: LCCN 2019910455 | ISBN 978-1-64633-788-0 (hardcover) | 978-0-57854-899-9 (paperback) | 978-1-64633-787-3 (eBook)
Subjects: LCSH Salvation--Christianity. | Theology. | BISAC RELIGION / Christian Theology / Soteriology | RELIGION / Christian Living / General | RELIGION / Biblical Studies / General | RELIGION / Christian Living / Spiritual Growth
Classification: LCC BT751.3 .H65 2019 | DDC 234.01/4--dc23

Translation Copyrights and Abbreviations

ERV-Scripture quotations are taken from the Holy Bible: Easy-to-Read Version. © 2014 by Bible League International. Used by permission.

ESV-Scripture quotations are from the ESV® Bible (The Holy Bible, English Standard Version®). Copyright © 2001 by Crossway, a publishing ministry of Good News Publishers. Used by permission. All rights reserved.

JUB-Jubilee Bible 2000. Copyright © 2013, 2020 by Ransom Press International. Used by permission. All rights reserved.

MSG-Scripture taken from The Message. Copyright © 1993, 1994, 1995, 1996, 2000, 2001, 2002. Used by permission of NavPress Publishing Group.

NIV-The Holy Bible, New International Version®. NIV®. Copyright © 1973, 1978, 1984, 2011 by Biblica, Inc.® Used by permission. All rights reserved worldwide.

NKJV-Scripture taken from the New King James Version®. Copyright © 1982 by Thomas Nelson. Used by permission. All rights reserved.

NLT-Scripture quotations are taken from the Holy Bible, New Living Translation. Copyright © 1996, 2004, 2015 by Tyndale House Foundation. Used by permission of Tyndale House Publishers, Inc., Carol Stream, Illinois 60188. All rights reserved.

TLB-Scripture quotations are taken from The Living Bible copyright © 1971. Used by permission of Tyndale House Publishers, Inc., Carol Stream, Illinois 60188. All rights reserved.

To my family, who always embodies unconditional love

Table of Contents

Preface ix
1 Why Do We Struggle? 1
2 Is There a Choice? 13
3 Should We Always Follow the Rules? 33
4 Are Christians Really Sinners? 57
5 Can God Forgive That Sin? 81
6 Will Future Sins Be Forgiven? 101
7 What is Our Cost Again? 121
8 What is In It for Me? 139
Epilogue: Yes...But 151
Acknowledgments .... a
About the Author c
Discussion Questions .... e
Scripture Index .... k

Preface

A LITTLE GIRL RAN INTO THE HOUSE and breathlessly asked her dad, "Where did I come from?" He felt his face flushing but steeled himself. He knew this would come someday. With a deep breath, he went into the detailed story of our physical beginnings. His daughter waited patiently although a bit shocked. When her father asked if she had any questions, she answered, "No, not really. I was wondering because our neighbors said they came from Ohio."

In this book I talk a fair amount about sin, which may be more than you really wanted to know on the subject. I would prefer not discussing sin at all. Instead, the focus should be on the freedom from sins Christians experience due to forgiveness through Christ Jesus. To appreciate the full impact of forgiveness, we must address both how we typically view sin and how the Bible does. If you are patient with me in the sin chapters, you will be rewarded in the forgiveness chapters.

There are quite a few Bible verses quoted in the book. I personally tend to skip over quotations when I read to avoid breaking the flow. Let me encourage you not to do as I do. I suggest the Scriptures themselves are very dynamic and often speak a strong message to us. Plus, I do not want this only to be about my opinions.

I use several different versions and paraphrases when quoting from the Bible. Translations should be accurate but also able to clearly communicate the meaning of the writer. Full accuracy and clarity cannot always be done using only a single version. Note that the use of a version in a particular instance does not make a judgment, one way or the other, on the quality of that version as a whole.

Not everyone is going to accept what I say without some concerns or objections. I do not need you to believe 100% of what I say but would be tickled with 65%. If I can get you to search the Scriptures to prove me wrong, then we will both be blessed. I just ask that you be open to the possibility that you might be wrong on some things, and I might be right.

My goal is not to repeat things you already know. Rather, I want to challenge you to think. I would be excited to hear I sparked a conversation or raised a question. Ultimately, though, I want you to see God's love is bigger than you previously imagined.

Gary L. Holmes

1 Why Do We Struggle?

> *Rodrigo Mendoza (slave trader and killer): "For me, there is no redemption."*
>
> *Father Gabriel: "God gave us the burden of freedom. You chose your crime. Do you have the courage to choose your penance? Do you dare do that?"*
>
> *Mendoza: "There is no penance, Father, for me."*
>
> *Gabriel: "But do you dare try it?"*
>
> *Mendoza: "Do I dare? Do you dare to see it fail?"*
>
> *(The Mission, Dir: Roland Joffé, Warner Brothers, 1986)*

RIGHT OUT OF COLLEGE, I was engaged in a brief enterprise that involved telephoning potential clients. My only memory of that endeavor came from one recording I heard. The answering machine simply stated: "You have reached the office of attorney John Doe. Please leave your contact information and whether you are guilty or not of the crime you just committed." Undoubtedly, that would be a shock to hear. Why would anyone want to hire a potential representative who assumed every caller was naturally a criminal? And yet, that exemplifies a perception of God held by a fair number of Christians. Many of us can imagine God answering our own inquiries: "HELL.....lo, this is the Lord. Please leave your name and state if you are guilty of the horrible sins that you have committed all your life." Put that way, it is understandable why most Christians might doubt their standing with their supposed Supreme Advocate.

Are we all guilty, all the time? We know guilt exists whenever any harm is done or whenever any crime is committed. On the other hand, guilt can be imagined, even when there has been no wrongdoing. For example, when confronted with some false accusation, many people have felt pangs of guilt because they might have done some bad deed unknowingly. It is also not uncommon for completely innocent people to confess to crimes, even severe ones, based on alleged proof or fierce accusations. In our courts, we are presumed to be innocent until proven guilty, but that is not always how it plays out. As one who has faced a court trial, I can assure you the entire judicial system runs more under the mentality of "smoke, therefore fire." After hours of grueling deposition and questioning on the stand, it is quite easy to doubt one's own innocence, even when the accused knows they did nothing wrong. That helps us understand why even victims can feel guilty. For example, robbery targets may accept some blame because they forgot to lock a door. Similarly, rape victims commonly suffer years thinking they were the ones who are at fault. Feelings from imagined guilt can be just as strong as those from real guilt. It is often hard to distinguish the difference. Given that blame attaches to innocent parties as well as to perpetrators, it is no surprise that felt guilt can become a default position for some people. That happens because we know we all are imperfect, make mistakes, and do harm at times. All people must have taken on real guilt at some point in their lives and likely most people have suffered imagined guilt as well.

For all our talk about freedom and forgiveness, Christians often live under a darker cloud of guilt feelings than do most non-Christians. This is because of our awareness of sin. If our real sins do not trip us up, perceived guilt piled on from countless sermons and lessons will. While we may not be ones who make regular trips to the mourner's bench or the confessional, perhaps we are dogged by feelings of inadequacies or doubts about our final destination. That is understandable, when preachers claim all Christians sin daily and we are all miserable sinners. We sing "Blessed Assurance" in church but afterward express hope we make it to heaven someday. Christians want to trust and believe despite recurring misgivings about God and salvation. Some theologians even tell us that doubt is a required part of our faith. If the burden from our own individual shortcomings is not enough, we sometimes believe we all must share in Adam's sin. Who wants to lead a Christian life dominated by such negative feelings?

Struggle to Be Righteous

This anxiety goes back deep in human history. There is an odd story in Genesis where Jacob wrestled all night with the angel of the Lord, likely a manifestation of Yahweh. The next morning the Lord seized Jacob and changed his name to Israel. The name Israel probably means he has struggled or strived with God. Jacob's descendants took on both the name and the meaning, so even today Christians often see themselves locked in a continuous struggle. What is the struggle? In broad terms, it is the battle for imperfect humans to have a relationship with a perfect God.

The problem begins with the disparate natures of the Creator and created. Because God is all-powerful and we are not, it is understandable why anyone wanting access to him would instinctively assume there is a huge gap to traverse. Historically, people have therefore sought a buffer or intermediary in between the Supreme Being and them. In pagan societies that might be second-tier gods, images, or idols. That explains why the mythical chief god in polytheistic societies has few dealings with humans. Any interaction between a divine being and humans almost always includes the necessary invention of lesser gods who have more frailties. Their faults make the sub-gods seem more relatable to mortals than some perfect being who likely has little concern for mere creatures. Christians are not exempt from this longing for a bridge. We turn to angels, Mary, dead saints, or even Jesus Christ to serve as mediators. The endless quest for a suitable intermediary illustrates well the seemingly unconquerable chasm between the Master of the Universe and us.

Happily, God does want to engage with us. As Paul walked among idols and altars built for various sub-gods, he spoke of the Lord of Heaven and Earth who created us so *"we could seek after God, and not just grope around in the dark but actually find him. He doesn't play hide-and-seek with us. He's not remote; he's near. We live and move in him, can't get away from him"* (Acts 17:27-28 MSG)! Unfortunately, any confidence felt in a potential relationship is tempered when we think about being face-to-face with God and what that might mean for us.

In the Bible, most human encounters with angels were frightening events. If meeting an angel elicited great anxiety, imagine what it might be like to experience any type of personal interaction with the creator of angels! You might recall the interesting story of Moses wanting to peek at God. Yahweh did not let Moses view the full glory but rather allowed Moses to look at his back, albeit with a warning, "*You cannot see my face, for no one may see me and live*" (Exodus 33:20 NIV). When Moses finally came down from the mountain, his face shone so brightly it had to be covered. No wonder people fear to be in the same room with God. Considering that we juxtapose such Bible stories with the theology we learn from movies, it is not surprising we fear our faces will melt in his presence.

Struggle with Sin

Sadly, it gets worse. The great divide between the Creator and us is not empty. Instead, a whole host of sin and evil bubbles up out of the canyon we wish to span. The prospect of crossing to the other side is daunting when we hear that God does not tolerate any wrongdoing because his eyes are too pure to even look at evil (Habakkuk 1:13). Preachers through the ages have amplified our dread: "The God that holds you over the pit of hell, much in the same way as one holds a spider, or some loathsome insect, over the fire, abhors you, and is dreadfully provoked; his wrath towards you burns like fire; he looks upon you as worthy of nothing else but to be cast into the fire; he is of purer eyes than to bear to have you in his sight" (Jonathan Edwards, *Sinners in the Hands of an Angry God*). Preaching has certainly softened since the time of Mr. Edwards but, somehow, Christians continue to face a frightening journey towards paradise.

We all get caught up in the misery. *"The Lord looks down from heaven on the children of man, to see if there are any who understand, who seek after God. They have all turned aside; together they have become corrupt; there is none who does good, not even one"* (Psalm 14:2-3 ESV). What are the chances of bridging the gap between a Sovereign God who cannot look at sin and every single person steeped in sin? Logic would suggest the odds to be slim. That is why we can understand much of the Old Testament pessimism about our prognosis, even if we have a lot of questions. Joshua, for example, sounded very ominous when he announced, *"You are not able to serve the Lord. He is a holy God; he is a jealous God. He will not forgive your rebellion and your sins. If you forsake the Lord and serve foreign gods, he will turn and bring disaster on you and make an end of you, after he has been good to you"* (Joshua 24:19-20 NIV). He may have had in mind this previous warning from Yahweh: *"And if you still won't listen to me or obey me, then I will let loose my great anger and send you seven times greater punishment for your sins. You shall eat your own sons and daughters, and I will destroy the altars on the hills where you worship your idols, and I will cut down your incense altars, leaving your dead bodies to rot among your idols; and I will abhor you"* (Leviticus 26: 27-30 TLB). All that can lead to dim hope indeed.

Our sense of helplessness may be taught to us, but more likely it is part of our DNA. All people have a need to be righteous with God. Christians and non-Christians alike

1 Why Do We Struggle?

can feel this distance between the Almighty and humans. Although professing salvation and forgiveness, many believers constantly experience the battle to stay the course. We want to be aligned with God, but sin keeps getting in the way. Just as a dieter awakens determined to eat well and then at night recalls the fleeting pleasure of a donut, many saints experience similar recurring regrets. Sin sits a few inches from our fingers, luring us with all kinds of tricks and enticements. Coupling our own desires with frightening thoughts of a deceiving devil, it is no wonder many Christians view life in terms of a constant struggle. Non-Christians may shiver at the mention of Satan, but likely it is believers who feel the full force of assertions like: "*Watch out for attacks from Satan, your great enemy. He prowls around like a hungry, roaring lion, looking for some victim to tear apart*" (1 Peter 5:8 TLB). It is little wonder we often feel there is no redemption and no way out of the cycle.

    The pessimism may be best exemplified in Paul's heart-rending confession "*I know that nothing good lives in me, that is, in my sinful nature. I want to do what is right, but I can't. I want to do what is good, but I don't. I don't want to do what is wrong, but I do it anyway. But if I do what I don't want to do, I am not really the one doing wrong; it is sin living in me that does it*" (Romans 7:18-20 NLT). This passage has spoken volumes to the hearts of Christians throughout time. We feel as if Paul has described in a few sentences the very core of our anxiety: a constant struggle to overcome sin, imperfection, and the ensuing feelings of guilt.

Were We Right about a Struggle?

For me, that anxiety started to shift one Sunday morning a few years ago. It is that change I want to share with you in this book and perhaps guide you towards a different, if not deeper, understanding about our Lord.

I had attended a lot of Bible classes over the years, but it has been rare that I have had an aha moment. That day, however, something clicked. Either by chance or by divine intervention, we were reading and discussing the very passage from Romans 7 above. I remember the teacher lamenting, "I am a sinner; I struggle with sin every day." I had heard that sentiment repeated many times over the years, and I certainly had expressed such ideas with similar conviction. When I heard my friend's confession, I was struck by novel thoughts: If we are all sinners and struggle daily with sin, then what is the point? Why are Christians battling with sin at all? If I must fight with sin every day, regardless of whether I am a Christian or not, then why even bother becoming a Christian in the first place? What advantage is there in hoping to be washed if I am still mired in the mud? The questions swirled. The thought of Christians claiming to be free from sin yet still admitting to a continuous struggle with sin suddenly seemed odd to me. It struck me at that moment as oxymoronic to be discussing any idea of "Christian sinners." Surely, I thought, we cannot be both Christian and sinner. Our class discussed the new ideas a bit, but most of my fellow members seemed resigned to enduring a constant struggle with sin. We had been taught that all our lives and it still seemed reasonable to most of us, despite some possible paradoxes.

Exploring Sin

The budding contrary thoughts I had were worrisome since they possibly conflicted with decades of belief that all Christians are sinners and remain locked in an on-going battle with sin. I had learned those things from fellow Christians and had even passed them on to others. For me, living with a little guilt in the tank seemed normal, maybe even helpful. That moment in class was not a time of doubt or anxiety about my core belief in God. Or was it? Was this some elephant in the room I had missed? Had I been wrong all along about some key idea? Is it possible we do not have to struggle with sin daily?

I spent the afternoon searching the Bible for the words sin, sinning, and sinner. I particularly wanted to see how these terms were applied to Christians, thinking that my earlier stray thoughts in the class were likely baseless. I discovered something remarkable, almost shocking: The Bible does not say as much about Christians sinning as I was expecting! Sure, there were warnings to avoid sin, but nothing that identified Christians as living in sin or being sinful. I could find almost nowhere in the Scriptures where a child of God is referred to as a sinner or even anything like it. In fact, what I found appeared to show the opposite.

Let me give a couple of examples, one from Paul and one from John. Paul opened his letter to the Colossian Christians by sharing that we have been delivered from darkness and transferred to the kingdom of the Son. This process of redemption comes through the forgiveness of sins. In contrast to the alienation from God in our pre-Christian life, *"now he has reconciled you by Christ's physical body through death to present you holy in his sight, without blemish and free from accusation—if you continue in your faith, established and firm, and do not move from the hope held out in the gospel*" (Colossians 1:22-23 NIV). Paul used powerful words to describe our present state: holy, without blemish, and blameless. While each of these words envisions a sense of sinlessness and purity, I want to touch on the second description. The idea of being without blemish is an Old Testament concept related to the sacrifices. Lamb sacrifices were to be unblemished or without defect (Exodus 12:5). In the New Testament, the metaphor is applied to Jesus Christ (1 Peter 1:19; Hebrews 9:14), who is clearly one without sin (1 Peter 2:22; Hebrews 4:15). That makes sense because sins would be blemishes. If we are without blemish, then it becomes problematic to continue viewing ourselves as being in sin. After all, "*What God has made clean, do not call common*" (Acts 10:15-16 ESV).

In another striking example of why it appears that Christians are not sinners, John said, *"No one who lives in him keeps on sinning. No one who continues to sin has either seen him or known him....No one who is born of God will continue to sin, because God's seed remains in them; they cannot go on sinning, because they have been born of God"* (1 John 3:6,9 NIV). I have no reason to doubt or question that I have been born of God, but John says that anyone born of God will not continue to sin. To discontinue something usually means to stop what you are doing. That would then mean John is saying that Christians stop sinning. A few translations even say we cannot sin when we are born of God! Of course, John could be using a figure of speech to make a point. Still, allowing for some hyperbole on his part or further study on our part, there is a strong indication that being a Christian and being a sinner are entirely two different things!

What does it mean that we are unblemished and do not continue to sin? Are we better than other people? Don't we still commit sins? Doesn't every sin make me a sinner? As a spoiler alert, the answers to these and many other questions have to do with what happens in Christ. Look back at what John had said earlier, "*You know that Jesus came to take away our sins, and there is no sin in him*" (1 John 3:5 NLT). Note there is no sin in Jesus Christ! We do not keep on sinning because we are in Christ and sin does not exist in him. We are without blemish because we share in the sacrifice of the Lamb.

2 Is There a Choice?

> Eleanor Shellstrop: "What? One in a million gets to live in paradise and everyone else is tortured for eternity? Come on. I wasn't...Gandhi, but I was okay. I was a medium person. I should get to spend eternity in a medium place, like Cincinnati. I mean, everyone who wasn't perfect but wasn't terrible should get to spend eternity in Cincinnati."
>
> Chidi Anagonye: "But apparently it doesn't work like that."
>
> (*The Good Place*, NBC, Pilot, 2017)

SIN IS A CHURCH WORD. It is not used much outside the context of religion. Unchurched people do not see themselves being in sin or committing sins. The world simply sees sin as a word Christians like to use for vice, crime, or wrongdoing. They turn words like sin, salvation, heaven, and hell over to us. Christians, on the other hand, often hear about sin. We believe we have a fairly good idea about what it is and how we should respond. Unfortunately, what we believe about sin and salvation does not always align with what we experience in real life. In other words, the problem is that we claim to be free from sin, yet we simultaneously claim we are strongly influenced by sin. I now believe we often misunderstand not only the nature of sin but also the forces that can free us from sin.

What we know about sin comes largely from three areas: 1. our experience, 2. what has been revealed to us by God through various means, and 3. what teachers, preachers, authors, and church leaders tell us. Hopefully, these three sources will all agree. It has been my experience that what the Bible teaches is not always reflected in the interpretations we hear. We should be open-minded enough to consider that there may be a disconnect at times between what the Bible says and what others think it says. When that happens, the Word should be the winner. Keep that in mind as we explore what the Bible teaches us about sin.

What God Does

Sin is a negative concept. By that I mean it is something we should not do in contrast to something we should do. If we want to understand what we should not do (i.e., sin) then we need to have a grasp of what we should do. Therefore, we need to know a little about God and why we are here.

Christians turn primarily to the Scriptures for their definitions and proof. Surprisingly, the Bible does not allocate much space trying to define God or even to prove his existence. One might expect those things would be the first goals attempted. However, the Bible does not start out by saying that God IS this or God IS that. Rather, it says, in the beginning, God DOES something. That pattern follows throughout the Bible. What we know about God comes primarily from what he does for us. His actions include creating, supporting, teaching, encouraging, disciplining, loving, judging, and saving.

2 Is There a Choice?

According to the story unfolded in the Word, what the Lord does for us elicits a response from us. We all respond, in one way or the other, to what he has done and is doing for us. We either are attracted to his actions and connected to him in some manner, or we are repelled by him and not with him. This choice is spoken of in many ways, but Jesus really made it clear when he said we either love God or we hate him. *"No one can serve two masters, for either he will hate the one and love the other, or he will be devoted to the one and despise the other"* (Matthew 6:24 ESV). That may seem awfully strong, but Jesus often used similar statements to make the point that our choice is definitely binary. We are for him or against him.

Why this dichotomy? Why can't we just be neutral? Cannot God just be a preference, like we treat a hobby? For instance, some people are passionate about birdwatching. Others cannot even imagine the appeal. Then there is a large contingent between these two groups who could not care less about birdwatching. The hobby elicits a wide range of attitudes and responses. In contrast, there is no disinterested or neutral state when it comes to God. We are either in the state of recognizing and appreciating what he does for us, or we are not. We cannot be in-between. Think of it like this. Suppose I ask if you believe in the abominable snowman. You could believe or not. You could also be in the middle somewhere, open to believing but not quite to the point of full belief. Your middle ground might just be complete disinterest, feeling that the existence or non-existence of the hairy beast does not affect your life one bit. Now suppose I ask if you believe there is a killer asteroid heading our way in three days. There is no middle ground in that scenario. You can believe it and act accordingly, or you can disbelieve and carry on with your life. You cannot remain indifferent. Possible immediate annihilation would demand action. It is the same with discussions about the Sovereign Deity. One cannot just believe in God as one believes in the existence of UFOs. If there truly is a God who created the cosmos and is bringing it fully under his dominion, our lives must be lived a certain way. We cannot stay neutral. We must believe and act, one way or the other.

The Either/Or Choices

With the Almighty, it is always an either/or decision rather than a buffet of options. This is described in several contrasting ways: love/hate, sheep/goats, good/evil, life/death, at home/away from home, light/darkness, freedom/slavery, heaven/hell, and spirit/sin. One of these either/or descriptions is described in terms of light with darkness as the opposite choice. For example:

- "*In the past, you were full of darkness, but now you are full of light in the Lord. So, live like children who belong to the light. This light produces every kind of goodness, right living, and truth*" (Ephesians 5:8-9 ERV).
- "*God is light, and there is no darkness in him at all*" (1 John 1:5 NLT).
- "*I am the light of the world. Whoever follows me will never walk in darkness will have the light of life*" (John 8:12 NIV).

2 Is There a Choice?

Light gives life and warmth, allowing us to function as living beings. We often view light as something and darkness as the opposite something. Note, however, darkness is not just an opposing force. In fact, darkness is not a force at all. In one sense, darkness does not even exist as a thing. It has no qualities or ingredients. It is not made up of anything. It cannot be examined and described except in terms of light, because darkness is simply the absence of light. There are basically two states we can be in. We can be in light. or we can be in darkness (or *not light*). On earth, we are seldom in total darkness. When we wake up in the middle of the night, we experience what we first think is this not light. After a few seconds, our eyes start to adjust, and we realize that there is, in fact, some light. The closest most of us come to total darkness is when we tour a cavern, and the guide turns out all the lights at some point. Assuming we do not panic, we stare and stare for a few minutes but see nothing! We feel what we think is darkness, but we cannot touch darkness. What we really experience is the state of not light.

Admittedly, there are different degrees of light around us, but that is not our point. Our point is that we can only be in one of two places at any single moment. In one place there is light, perhaps limited light, but light, nonetheless. In the other place, there is no light. The Bible claims that God is light. That is not literally true. He is not some big light bulb or super sun. Light signifies his glory and that he is the source of all life. Applying the light metaphor, we can say there is either God or *not God*. Depending on our choice and relationship we are in a state with God or in a state without God. We think in terms of a spiritual state or position rather than a physical place. It is true the Bible does use physical descriptions for spiritual concepts. For example, the Lord is described as sitting on a throne in a place called heaven. We know that God does not have a physical body that is seated, nor does he live in a specific place. In the same way, we may talk of being in a heavenly city or walking with God. Those are merely human terms for being in the God state. In contrast, the state of being without God might be referred to as being in hell or a pit. Again, that would be a spiritual state of not God rather than a physical location.

We can argue why there is even a not God state. Suffice it to say that God gave us a choice and the only way we can have a choice is that we must be able to choose not God. A professor once said hell was one of God's greatest gifts to us. That seemed extreme to me until I realized allowing another person freedom to leave a relationship requires more love than forcing them to stay. The Lord gave us a tremendous gift when he gave us the option to choose hell, or not God. He certainly could have programmed us to always choose him and always to be perfect. In that case, we would be more machine and less human. The fact is the Creator did bless us with the ability to choose, change, and grow. Unfortunately, freedom comes with a host of problems because many choose unwisely. When that happens, we experience the resulting pain, suffering, and evil that comes from poor choices.

As you know, the problem of evil has been a subject of much philosophy and theology for a long time. The dilemma is commonly formed in a question: How can a good but all-powerful God allow evil in this world? While there is much debate, the simplest explanation is choice. If we are to have free will, there must be a choice of evil or not God. Of course, non-believers love to throw the evil card out as a reason not to believe in God. That is absurd since there is no problem if there is no God. Non-believers never seem to get that.

The Choice of Hell

As an aside, there is a thought that anyone who winds up in hell knows his or her destination going in and will not be surprised. Why is that? Because hell is, in simplest terms, where God is not. If you do not choose God, then you must know you will not be with him. *The Great Divorce* imagines people in hell having a regular opportunity to board a bus and visit heaven. If they like, they can even stay in heaven. In the end, after walking around for a while, the condemned board the bus again and return to hell. That makes sense because they chose not God in the first place. The view that people would prefer hell is more likely than the view I grew up believing. We always thought that no one wanted to be in hell, and we would all kill, so to speak, to get out of there. I assumed everyone preferred God and heaven, but apparently, that is not the case. Lewis noted, "There are only two kinds of people in the end: those who say to God, 'Thy will be done,' and those to whom God says, in the end, 'Thy will be done.' All that are in Hell, choose it. Without that self-choice, there could be no Hell. No soul that seriously and constantly desires joy will ever miss it. Those who seek find. Those who knock it is opened" (C. S. Lewis, *The Great Divorce*, 1946).

God or Not God

We can choose God, or we can choose not God. From those two choices, come the notions of good and bad. In the Bible, God is good and the source of good because he is the instigator of life and the source of life. Where there is no light there is darkness (or not light). In the same way, where there is no life, there is death (or not life). Finally, where there is no good there is evil (or not good).

We come from God and our origins are in God, so God considered creation to be good, particularly the creation of humans. We were made in the image of the Creator so share certain God-like qualities. This image of God means we are linked to him in a relationship. Peter called this relationship a sharing of God's divine nature. *"Everything that goes into a life of pleasing God has been miraculously given to us by getting to know, personally and intimately, the One who invited us to God. The best invitation we ever received! We were also given absolutely terrific promises to pass on to you— your tickets to participation in the life of God"* (2 Peter 1:3-4 MSG).

We are not gods of any kind and therefore do not have all of God's qualities. In addition, any God-like qualities we do possess are not held to the same degree God does. We are not able to fashion the cosmos or know all things. On the other hand, we were created to share in and own many of the other qualities of the Savior. Biblical lists of God-like qualities often culminate in love. *"Add to your faith goodness; and to goodness, knowledge; and to knowledge, self-control; and to self-control, perseverance; and to perseverance, godliness; and to godliness, mutual affection; and to mutual affection, love. For if you possess these qualities in increasing measure, they will keep you from being ineffective and unproductive in your knowledge of our Lord Jesus Christ"* (2 Peter 1:5-8 NLT). We were created to be like the Lord by acting as he does. When we act as he would act, by showing love and kindness, then we are said to be good. When we act in other ways, we are said to be evil, or not good. That is not because we are good in our core or bad in our core. Rather, it has to do with the state in which we choose to live. We can live within those God-like qualities that reflect his image or we can abandon them and be something entirely different. Of course, this is only possible through the work of God. *"Without these qualities you can't see what's right before you, oblivious that your old sinful life has been wiped off the books"* (2 Peter 1:9 MSG).

Earlier we said that sin was a negative concept in that it was more about what we do not do, rather than what we do. Here is why. Darkness and death are not actually things and can only be defined in terms of not light and not life. Continuing the thought, evil (or bad) is not actually a thing but can only be defined in terms of not good. Sin works in much the same way. Being in sin is not being in a place or location; rather, it is the state of being away from the Creator. Sin is anything that keeps us from being with God or can keep us from him. At its center, sin is rebellion. *"It's your sins that have cut you off from God. Because of your sins, he has turned away and will not listen anymore"* (Isaiah 59:2 NLT). Sin is what moves us into the not God state because sin is acting against the King and his dominion. We can also say that sin is acting differently from the way the Lord or someone in his image would act. Rebellion is opposition to authority. In this case, it is the choice of not God manifested in a life of sin. Sin is not an outside force of evil that causes us to do things against our will. Rather, sin is the option we select instead of God. Sometimes that is open, defiant opposition and, at other times, it is the displacement of God from our lives. Always, sin involves the choice to be away from God.

Eternal Punishment

Discussions about God will invariably drift to the not God side of the equation. Such chats would include concerns about hell, damnation, and punishment. Few people like to deal with unpleasant topics and hell is about as unpleasant as one can imagine. Eternal damnation is a Biblical reality that cannot be denied by Christians and should be explainable without appearing arrogant or judgmental. Of course, that is easier said than done. As an example, the innocent assertion that I am bound for heaven can easily be misconstrued. It might imply I am doing what it takes to get to heaven, while you are not doing the same. It follows by deduction you must be going to hell. Surely no one wants to hear that, even if that person believes in neither heaven nor hell.

When we talk about actions and the corresponding relationship to heaven or hell, we invariably talk about the notions of good and bad. Metaphors like light and darkness seldom express fully what we want to know. Instead, the two most common concerns are expressed in terms of good and bad. They might not be the right questions to ask, but they are ubiquitous. Some God-believers ask, "How can we be good enough to earn a final reward and avoid punishment for being too bad?" Some God-deniers ask, "How can a good God create and send people to a bad hell?" Let us deal with the question from God-believers first.

Good, Better, and Best

It is popularly accepted among those who acknowledge life after death that being good gets one to some form of heaven, nirvana, or paradise. Conversely, being bad gets one into something akin to hell or into some form of non-existence. In fact, most religions teach exactly that. Christianity, for the most part, officially tries to deny that belief, but I contend a majority of Christians feel good/bad behavior directly affects our ultimate destination. We certainly live that way.

Complicating the somewhat simple belief that good results in going to heaven and bad results in going to hell is the fact that good or bad behavior is not easily defined. Quickly, we realize that there are varying degrees of both. Yes, we might conclude, really bad people go one way and really good people the other. What about those in between? Where is the line drawn? Who decides? The complication of defining and judging behavior forces us to insert a dynamic, progressive model into what seems to be a binary scenario. What that means is we must fit a square peg into a round hole. For the results (destination), we often accept an either/or scenario. Some people go to heaven, and some go to hell. For the cause (our journey of behavior), we likely believe in a kind of linear/comparative progression. In other words, although we might accept that the choice of destination is the two-fold destination of a good place or a bad place, those of us moving in one of those directions usually think we are strung out on a long continuum. Let me try to explain this graphically.

Imagine a line. At one end is heaven, or God, and at the other end hell. I would add Satan at the hell end, but you must remember Satan is not a god in equal opposition to God nor is he the ruler of hell. He is a created being that will receive his own consequences. As most of us think, humans are somewhere on that line, some better than others and some closer to heaven than others. We view our chance of reaching the best end by how good we are. The better we are, in comparison to the others on the line, the better our chances. And it works that way, so we often believe, in our life. We want to improve at being good in order to increase the odds of reaching our goal. We all would like to think we are well along on the goodness line. After all, everyone thinks they are better than average. Averages and comparisons can be worrisome. Remember that about half the people are always below average in whatever one is measuring. In any group of people, half are below average in beauty, wealth, intelligence, athletic ability, etc. That also means half would be below average in good deeds. You or I could even be in that bottom half of such a goodness scale. That might be worrisome, given Jesus' words: "*The gate to hell is very wide, and there is plenty of room on the road that leads there. Many people go that way*" (Matthew 7:13 ERV).

Wanting to Be Good

Are we then striving to be good and to get better to please God, so he will let us through the pearly gates? The easy theological answer is to say that goodness has nothing to do with salvation. This position is especially common among Protestants, whose very existence is founded on the notions that we do not merit salvation and that there is nothing we can do to earn it. In typical Protestant theology, if salvation comes, it does so through the grace of God. This mostly goes back to Martin Luther whose key theme was "*The righteousness of God is revealed from faith for faith, as it is written, 'The righteous shall live by faith'*" (Romans 1:17 ESV). In my opinion, Ephesians is even clearer on this point than Romans: "*For it is by grace you have been saved, through faith—and this is not from yourselves, it is the gift of God— not by works, so that no one can boast*" (Ephesians 2:8-9 NIV). Luther argued we cannot earn salvation or pay for it through our own goodness. Since we are saved by grace and not through our goodness, it is irrelevant how good we are. Goodness gets a person nowhere when it comes to obtaining salvation or reaching heaven.

While that is the easy answer in some respects, it is not always a satisfying one for many of us. There are a few reasons for that. It can sound like doing good or being good is not especially important. Also, while Christians often acknowledge that we are saved by grace and that we cannot earn salvation by being good, the fact is we still find it hard to accept and believe. Some who insist salvation is only by grace can be the very ones who work the hardest to get their salvation. Finally, while it seems noticeably clear in the New Testament that salvation is a gift and that heaven comes through grace, there are also a lot of other passages which seem to say just as clearly that goodness and performing good works do count for something. As an example, James wrote,

"So you see, it isn't enough just to have faith. You must also do good to prove that you have it. Faith that doesn't show itself by good works is no faith at all—it is dead and useless. But someone may well argue, 'You say the way to God is by faith alone, plus nothing; well, I say that good works are important too, for without good works you can't prove whether you have faith or not; but anyone can see that I have faith by the way I act'" (James 2:17-18 TLB). Incidentally, Luther thought the book of James so opposite of grace that he called it a letter of straw. Regardless, Jesus seemed to support James when he said in the parable of the sheep and the goats that the kingdom would be inherited by those who fed the hungry, cared for the sick, and visited those in prison (Matthew 25:31-46). That can sound very much like a need to do good things to obtain our salvation.

This last reason does leave us with the question of whether goodness counts towards gaining heaven, or it does not. If we can figure out the seeming contradiction of faith or works (gift or compensation) then we would go a long way towards solving hundreds of years of Christian controversy. I have enough naivety to think I might have part of the solution. Let us revisit the passage in Ephesians 2. Clear reasoning as to why goodness does not result in our salvation was laid out by Paul in verses 8-9, as we noted earlier. In the same breath, however, he added this: *"For we are God's handiwork, created in Christ Jesus to do good works, which God prepared in advance for us to do"* (Ephesians 2:10 NIV). Paul was saying good works do not save us, but good works are what we were created to do. What is the deal? Does "being good" help us get to heaven or does it not? Is goodness necessary, or merely helpful, in our quest?

The answer is that verse 10 is not presenting a difficult contradiction but is presenting the solution to the questions. Paul says we were created for good works. We were created to be good just as God is good. That is our purpose. It is not the means to the end; it is the end! That is huge. Being good is not what we do to get somewhere. It is where we all need to go. Acting good is for all people and not just Christians. Everyone was created for that very purpose. It is no wonder that degrees of goodness can often be seen in most people.

Think about the lowly toaster. As far as I can tell, it has a singular purpose. If it is toasting bread, it is fulfilling that purpose and being what it was made to be. If it breaks and no longer toasts, then we agree it is not fulfilling its *raison d'être*. It might even be said that it is no longer a toaster. If we repair the broken appliance, then we have brought it back to its true nature. It has not gained anything more. It has simply had its purpose restored back to its original state. In the same way, all people are created for good works. We were all made to love God and love our neighbors. If we deviate from that nature through sin (i.e., the choice of sin) we quit fulfilling our nature. If God repairs or restores us to love and goodness, then we simply are back to where we began. Being good is not how we obtain a relationship with God on earth or in heaven. Rather, our relationship back with God allows us to obtain goodness. I repeat: Being good is not the means to the end but is the end. Being good does not get us salvation. Salvation allows us to be fully what we were created for, viz., being good.

Good People and Hell

Earlier we said there were two wide-spread questions, one from God-believers and one from God-deniers. The first question often coming from God-believers asked, "How can we be good enough to earn a final reward and avoid punishment for being too bad?" We answered that by saying being good gets neither the Christian nor the non-Christian to heaven. That probably also answers the question some God-deniers ask, "How can a good God create and send people to a bad hell?" However, that answer may be somewhat inadequate for those who propose the latter question. We will, therefore, take a supplemental approach.

Here is the problem. Non-Christians recognize quite clearly that most Christians teach a rather exclusive view which comes from the Bible. *"Jesus said to him, 'I am the way, and the truth, and the life. No one comes to the Father except through me'"* (John 14:6 ESV). If those people who are not Christ-followers were all ax murderers, serial killers, rapists, and traitors, this implied banishment to the nether world would be recognized as somewhat fair by most of the world's population, theists, atheists, and agnostics alike. That is not the case. In fact, the consensus must be that there are a lot of folks outside the boundaries of Christianity who would be considered decent, law-abiding, and good people. What about them? Is it possible that good people are going to hell? If the answer to that is yes, then many people will not only reject that conclusion as unacceptable but will disavow any notion of a God who might affirm it. The questions are myriad, but in the simplest terms, we will concentrate on an example of one question that is ubiquitous: If a person is an atheist (God-disbeliever) or an agnostic (God-doubter) who is also a good citizen, how can a good God consign that person to an eternal, fiery punishment?

I have heard Christians try to answer the question by saying that God is sovereign and can do what he wants. Others claim God is, by definition, fair and just so, therefore, anything he does is acceptable. However, while there might be truth to those answers, I do not think they necessarily are completely satisfactory in most cases. We will be benefited by discussing further the concepts of choice and acceptance.

Goodness may be in the eyes of the beholder, but I think that there is a consensus that a good person would be one who, for the most part, either treats others well or, in the reverse, does not treat them badly. The recognizable qualities would be much like the Scout's list: trustworthy, loyal, helpful, friendly, courteous, and kind. Given that, we would have to acknowledge that there are "good" people who are not Christians or God-followers. To be honest, likely there are many non-Christians who are better at being good than I am and, perhaps, than you are. Are they then bound for heaven or, a forbidden thought, further up the line towards getting their ticket stamped than we are?

Sign Up and Play

In our earlier discussion of sin, we talked a bit about the choice of God versus the choice of not God. How does that choice take place? Unfortunately, among Christians, there is still disagreement and debate about the particulars. In a broad sense, we can say that the Bible teaches us that choosing God involves two things: acknowledgment and participation. That should not surprise us. Alignment with almost any organization or group will involve, in some form or the other, these two elements. Furthermore, probably any on-going relationship demands the same. The first is a commitment, desire, and decision to be a part of the group (even a group of two). The second is the actual doing of the things that the group does. Think about the local softball team. We can say that here the acknowledgment and participation is manifest in the simple formula, sign up and play. We cannot just show up whenever we want and expect to play. We usually must do a sign-up to signal our wish to be on the team. Also, we recognize, signing up is not enough to make us a part of the team. We also must show up and play. If a person signs up but never plays, then no one would say that person was a team member. Our best designation might be a no-show. It is the same with God. There must be the dual implementation of sign up and play; one alone does not work. The acknowledgment (or sign up) would be the commitment demonstrated, often publicly, by faith, confession of that faith, and baptism. Those are all expressions of the desire to move into (or back into) relationship with God. The participation (or play) would be characterized by repentance which involves moving from a life of sin and into a life of love. Some of us may be better at loving than others, just as some of us may be better at softball than others. The thing is to play.

Therefore, the question should not be about the level of goodness for the non-Christian (or the Christian, for that matter). Instead, the better question is: Has the atheist, agnostic, and otherwise non-Christian signed up to have a relationship with God? Have they made a commitment that signals a desire to not just love their neighbor (i.e., be good) but also to love God with all their heart, all their soul, and all their mind? We do not have to answer those questions for anyone else nor do we need to feel guilty for condemning others, which we do not mean to do. Our choice to be Christian says nothing about our being better than anyone else. It also does not say anything about how good or bad are non-Christians, thereby implying whether they will go to heaven or to hell. Our choice to be a Christian is simply our choice to live as we, and all peoples, were made to live. Another person's choice will be between the Lord and him or her. We can share the reasons for our choice and even encourage others to do the same, but we cannot make the choice for another person.

We like to define sin as bad behavior and sins as specific acts of bad behavior. Although there is some truth to those definitions, we have shown that sin involves not just behavior but also a choice. By thinking of sin only in terms of behavior we fall into the trap that our primary choice is simply between good and bad behavior. The choice is not between good and bad behavior. Instead, the choice is always between God and not God. There is no Cincinnati or middle ground. When we choose not God we choose to be in sin, because sin is what opposes God or is contrary to his nature. When we choose God, we choose to cease continuing in sin, because there is no sin in God.

3 Should We Always Follow the Rules?

> **The Archangel Michael:** "Remember what John and Paul said."
>
> **Frank Quinlan:** "The apostles?"
>
> **Michael:** "No, the Beatles. All you need is love."
>
> (*Michael*, Dir: Nora Ephron, New Line Distribution, 1996)

WE HAVE TWO POSSIBLE POSITIONS OR STATES, as we discussed. We can be a part of God or not a part of God. We have said that being a part of God means that we are in a relationship with him in some manner. Obviously, this relationship between the Creator and creation is not the same as the relationship we experience with other human beings. After all, it is not often God has visited with and communicated directly with a human. How directly the Father answers prayers and how much he interacts in our daily lives is a continuing subject of debate. In the same way, the mysterious work of angels or the Holy Spirit can elicit a wide variety of opinions among Christians. Many of us would be surprised at how often the brothers and sisters differ in how and how much God works in our lives. For our purposes, it will suffice to say the Lord does take an interest in us by responding at times to our prayers. We also believe that he created us in some manner and had a purpose for doing so. By attributing human emotions to God, we can say he enjoys our interactions with him and appreciates our worship. He shares happiness in our discoveries, our creativity, and our learnings. He also wants us to act in a certain way, especially as that relates to our fellow human beings. The Lord appreciates our growing in and exhibiting such attributes as love, kindness, patience, forgiveness, and acceptance. In a simple way we can say our part of the relationship consists of:

- Recognizing God as our Maker and Sovereign Master of Creation,
- Acknowledging God through worship and thanksgiving,
- Using the resources provided by him to live productive lives, and
- Treating the rest of creation as the Lord has treated us.

I made up this summary, but I think you get the point. It is an extremely brief survey of what it means to be a part of God and have a relationship with him. On the flip side, we can say that the opposite of being with God will involve beliefs or actions contrary to the four things mentioned above. In other words, the path away from the Lord will involve one or all the following:

- Not recognizing God as our Maker and Sovereign Master of Creation,

- Not acknowledging God through worship and thanksgiving,
- Not using the resources provided by him to live productive lives, or
- Not treating the rest of creation as the Lord has treated us.

Earlier we said that sin is doing anything that separates us from God or can lead to separation from God. That is true, but the above choices are the broad areas that lead us to be apart from the Lord. Looking at these four main areas of sin does not give us the specifics we need to understand and avoid sin. To do that we have to further break down sin into parts. These components are the specific actions or non-actions that we commonly refer to as sins. Remember that for separation from God to happen, a choice on our part is needed. That choice may be deliberate, or the choice can be less direct. Regardless of our stated intentions, following any of the four negative paths above puts us in the opposite direction from God and will, in fact, lead us to separation from him. Remember the son in the famous parable. He left home and was no longer a part of the family. It does not clearly tell us why. Did he hate his father and desperately want to get out of the house? Or did he simply want to be his own person and start a new life down the road? His reasoning really does not matter because it was his actions that caused him to choose a path that led away from home. The specific behavior of bad choices or committing sins embodied and proved his rebellion.

Principled Law and Rule Laws

To understand what is meant by sins we must know something of laws and rules. Paul often tied the concept of law with that of sin (Romans 7:5, 10-11; 8:1-2). However, avoiding sin and knowing what is right to do is not always simply following the rules. Let us consider an analogy. Would it be wrong for a person to walk into the street in front of my house? Would that be a misdemeanor? Generally, we would say no, because there is not a law in my community that says stepping into a street is forbidden. In addition, few people would say that the act is unethical or immoral. Yet, the questions are not always easy to answer. Each time a variable changes, the answer to our first question about wrongdoing must be modified. For example, does it matter if the said pedestrian is in a crosswalk or not? Does our answer change if we know the street is cordoned off for repairs or a 5K run? What if the person walking in the street were struck by a car at night and the car had no headlights? Should the streetwalker be the only one at fault? What if the person walking out into the street was a three-year-old? Would that be wrong? Would the child be scolded or punished even if no cars were approaching?

I use the relatively non-controversial action of walking in the street to illustrate the complexity of defining wrongdoing or sin. It is impossible to say that walking in the street is absolutely wrong or absolutely right. It is equally impossible to say that following the law gives us all our answers. It depends on the circumstances and who is doing an action and for what reason. I am not here to decide all the rules and laws associated with walking in the street. I believe, though, we can learn a few lessons about wrong and about sin.

As a rule (no pun intended), laws are made to protect against unwanted consequences or harm of some kind. Of course, we realize that bad rules and laws are enacted out of ignorance, evil, or greed. There are two ways to approach the potential problem of walking in the street. We might say, "The street can be a very dangerous place so please be careful before going into the street or allowing your children to do the same." Alternatively, we can create a whole raft of laws and rules dealing with how and when a pedestrian can be in the street.

The first approach is based on principles and the second approach is based on rules. Both approaches figure significantly in how we do law which governs our own actions and the interactions we have with others. Broadly speaking, we usually see principles as the general, fundamental code of conduct that motivates us internally to act a certain way. Rules, on the other hand, are more specific and control us externally. While principles and rules work differently, they are not mutually exclusive. Rather, they often work in tandem for the same ends. That applies to God's laws as well as to societal laws.

For our purposes, we will call the first method *principled law* and the second method *rule laws*. In one sense, it does not matter which approach you choose as it really gets down to the same goal. In our example, that end would be protecting people from getting killed in the street. We recognize that principled law is much simpler and less burdensome generally than rule laws. Most of us would say that the principled law approach is preferable in most scenarios of life. It is the idea that acting prudently results in doing the least amount of harm. Because some people act out of ignorance (children, for example) or some people act out of selfishness ("I can walk wherever and whenever I want, and other people need to move out of the way"), rule laws must come into play. As a result, the more rules we make the more we must make to explain the first rules. Laws proliferate when people congregate. Regardless of how many rules exist, we typically just want people to act unselfishly and reasonably. One person may respond more to rule laws and one person may respond more to principled law, but the goal is safety and protection for all.

God's Rule Laws

It is important that we realize it is the same with God. He did not make up a bunch of rule laws at creation just to annoy us. In fact, it appears he started out with almost no list or, at best, a list consisting of one or two rules. As the world grew and circumstances changed, rules and laws began to multiply. Sometimes those rules came from the Sovereign Lord and sometimes from humans. At times, the laws were the same between God's law and people's laws. At other times, they were different and sometimes were even in opposition. In God's case and mostly in peoples' cases, rules and laws were enacted due to people's ignorance or selfishness. Such rules are aids to help us make easier choices. The law says to do this, so we do this. The law says do not do that, so we do not do that. Decisions about proper behavior are then simplified. *"The law was like those Greek tutors, with which you are familiar, who escort children to school and protect them from danger or distraction, making sure the children will really get to the place they set out for*" (Galatians 3:24 MSG). Rules become guides for proper behavior.

Earlier we said that sin is anything that keeps us from being with God or can keep us from him. That is not specific enough. When it comes to daily living, most of us need something more concrete. We prefer to know: This is a sin, or that is not a sin. Typically, it follows in our thinking that rules are the key to recognizing specific sins. Laws and rules do not cause sin, but Paul explained, "*Why, then, was the law given? It was given alongside the promise to show people their sins*" (Galatians 3:19 NLT). He added, "*It was the law that showed me my sin. I would never have known that coveting is wrong if the law had not said, 'You must not covet*'" (Romans 7:7 NLT). Thus, rules point out what is bad behavior or sin.

We typically believe that when we follow God's rules, we are good. When we do not, we are bad. In Santa Claus terms, it is how we know who is naughty or nice. James made the connection between law and sin when he discussed sinning: "*You are guilty of breaking God's law*" (James 2:9 NIV). On the face, these verses seem to support the idea that breaking the rule laws is sinful and keeping the rule laws saves us. We often see the Lord as a supreme rule-maker. If you follow his rules, you are okay. If you do not, look out! We sometimes hear, "God said such-and-such and that settles it!" Unfortunately, it is not always that simple with any laws and that applies to God's laws as well. To see why that is so, we need to answer a couple of questions: Are God's laws absolute? Are God's laws necessary?

Limits on Rule Laws

A stop sign has no meaning unless placed in the context of traffic flow. If people are always willing to be considerate in taking turns, then most stop signs could be discarded. I once correctly stopped at a stop sign, only to have an accident when I moved into the intersection. The problem resulted when the other person did not stop at his stop sign. Yes, the fault was his. However, in honesty, I could have prevented the accident if I had been paying more attention to driving and less attention to following the rule. I am not saying the stop sign was bad nor am I saying we should run stop signs. Not at all. I am saying that stop signs are only helpful as an aid to good defensive driving. We can install all the stop signs we want, but we cannot rely solely on them in all scenarios. In the same way, laws are generally good. They are not the end but only the means to the end. Rule laws, even Biblical laws, do not and cannot cover every situation.

For example, in his letter, James dealt with a public worship situation in which rich folks are given more prestigious seating than are poor folks. James said, "*It is good when you obey the royal law as found in the Scriptures: 'Love your neighbor as yourself.' But if you favor some people over others, you are committing a sin. You are guilty of breaking the law. For the person who keeps all the laws except one is as guilty as a person who has broken all of God's laws. For the same God who said, 'You must not commit adultery,' also said, 'You must not murder.' So, if you murder someone but do not commit adultery, you have still broken the law*" (James 2:8-11 NLT). Here James did what we said happens all the time. He created a new rule law using what we commonly call case law. As far as I know, there is no place in the Bible before James' letter that says, "Thou shalt not give rich people a better seat in worship than poor people." Despite no prior law, James said that if you do discriminate you are breaking the law and committing sin. Is he referring to the law he just created? No, James says people break the principled law of neighbor love by breaking the specific rule of non-discrimination in worship. The problem is not that we might break a rule; the problem is not loving our neighbor. Did favoritism only become a sin once it was written down by James? Of course not. All he did was clarify by a rule law something that was wrong all along. It was wrong to show favoritism before a rule law was ever written down explicitly because favoritism is not what God-like creatures do. We love our neighbor as ourselves and therefore do not discriminate in worship, whether there is a written rule law or not. The point is the Bible does not give us a specific rule or law for every occasion. The Lord never intended us to have a rule for everything. Specific rule laws are useful, but they cannot be relied upon to guide us in all circumstances. They are limited. They pop up and change from situation to situation.

Are God's Laws Absolute?

You might ask, "Aren't God's laws absolute and eternal?" If you are talking about a principled law (or royal law as James calls it) such as love your neighbor, then the answer is yes. If you are talking about a rule law, then the answer is likely no. James' law which forbids the seating of rich people ahead of poor people was not even spelled out for most of human history. Rule laws can come and go. For example, earlier the Lord was truly clear that he wanted his people to offer animal sacrifices. Guess what? I do not know a single Christian who practices or encourages animal sacrifice today. If animal sacrifice in the Jerusalem temple was absolute law, then a whole bunch of people for the last two thousand years are in trouble. The list of laws set up by God but now ignored or obsolete includes things like wearing phylacteries, observing the festival of trumpets, and not eating pork or screech owls. We are not talking merely about man-made laws; we are talking about God-given laws that we do not follow because we have decided they are not universal and immutable. Is there anywhere in the Bible God said it is okay to ignore the festival of trumpets? No, humans quit participating on their own. It is not just God who changes his rule laws.

If God intended to supply us a list of absolute laws as our basis of salvation, then we would have to believe the list would be comprehensive. It is not though. A whole host of issues we deal with today are not even specifically addressed in the Scriptures. There are no direct mentions of abortion, drug addiction, sex slavery, or child abuse, to name a few. Rule laws can only cover so many situations. We always must rely on principled law to cover everything else. That is not a bad thing. We will all love more fully when we are "touched by the better angels of our nature" per Abraham Lincoln, rather than merely guided by a list of rules.

We aren't just talking about trivial or minor laws. Some of the most foundational laws in the world are the Ten Commandments. We still like to engrave them in granite and display them as monuments for all times. And yet, few Christians observe the Sabbath as a day of rest from work. That is perhaps surprising since it is number four on the greatest hits list. Jesus healed on the Sabbath. He picked and ate grain on the Sabbath. Although he normally observed the Sabbath, he also recognized that even a Ten Commandment law had its limits and was not absolute. That is why Jesus said, "*The Sabbath was made to meet the needs of people, and not people to meet the requirements of the Sabbath*" (Mark 2:27 NLT). Jesus clearly was attesting that even God's rules are not absolute in and of themselves. Understand what Jesus meant when he said people were not put on this earth for the purpose of following commandments. The most important thing is the goal and not the means to the goal. Law loses its power and purpose if one loses sight of the goal.

Changes to Rule Laws

How can some Christians say God's rule laws are eternal, even though human rule laws do change? The most common argument is that God's laws are eternal unless or until he changes them. This view assumes humans cannot change one of God's rule laws. The argument posits the notion rule laws in the Old Testament were simply replaced by ones in the New Testament because God either changed his mind or was following a certain plan. It is believed the New Testament law overlapped quite a bit with the Old Testament law, eliminating specific rules while adding others.

This whole idea has many problems. One, it is difficult to prove God's rule laws are eternal when this argument concedes some rule laws ceased. How can rule laws be eternal when they are not? Two, there is no clear Biblical support for the idea God wanted to create a new set of rule laws and get rid of an old set. Jesus and New Testament writers refer to Old Testament rules all the time. Jeremiah and Hebrews do talk about a new covenant, but those discussions have to do with promises of the Spirit and do not mention a new set of rules. There are many questions about how, why, and when this supposed law replacement happened. Three, this idea assumes all changes, additions, and subtractions of rule laws always come from God. There are many examples of law changes for which we have nothing in the Bible about God approving. These would include the institution of synagogues, use of wine at Passover, and the elimination of the Year of Jubilee. Plus, we know humans did make modifications and that we are encouraged to make interpretations concerning laws. Jesus talked a lot about such things. All of us make decisions about which Bible laws to follow and which we do not. Are we certain about which Old Testament laws remained valid and which became obsolete? Are we in agreement about which New Testament laws are to be followed? Four, this argument only tries to keep alive the myth that keeping rule laws is the aim and the way to salvation. The New Testament is clear that we are not under rule laws. Paul noted: *"If you are led by the Spirit, you are not under the law"* (Galatians 5:18 ESV). Paul never said we are not under the old list of laws because we are under a new replacement list! Rather, he affirmed life in the Spirit contrasts with all rule laws, even God-given ones. Our freedom does not involve following a new set of rule laws.

Consider a good example that shows that God's rule laws are not always universal and eternal. Circumcision was a law that predated the law given through Moses. It was a key element for God's people. Despite that, Paul said circumcision is not a requirement for all people and for all times. At one point he stated, "*It doesn't matter whether we have been circumcised or not*" (Galatians 6:15 NLT). To say a law given by God and a cornerstone in God's relationship with his people is merely optional is incredible. Paul did not stop there. He audaciously added that for some people circumcision is forbidden! He exclaimed, "*Mark my words! I, Paul, tell you that if you let yourselves be circumcised, Christ will be of no value to you at all*" (Galatians 5:2 NIV). Paul was not knocking circumcision for he himself was circumcised and he even had his co-worker Timothy circumcised. Rather, he was making the same point as James by saying that rule laws, such as circumcision, find meaning only in the greater goals of principled law. He clarified this a bit more in Romans when he shared, "*Circumcision, the surgical ritual that marks you as a Jew, is great if you live in accord with God's law. But if you don't, it's worse than not being circumcised. The reverse is also true: The uncircumcised who keep God's ways are as good as the circumcised—in fact, better. Better to keep God's law uncircumcised than break it circumcised*" (Romans 2:25-27 MSG). Circumcision, like all rule laws, is situationally related to bigger purposes. Instead of concentrating solely on the act itself, Paul thought the bigger play was to follow the principled law which deals directly with our relationship with God, i.e., "*whether we have been transformed into a new creation*" (Galatians 6:15 NLT). Rule laws only get us where we want to be if they are in the context of principled law. "*Circumcision is circumcision of the heart, by the Spirit, not by the written code*" (Romans 2:29 NIV). Rule laws serve a specific purpose in certain situations and times. Few of them would be truly eternal and universal. Governments, churches, and individuals are constantly creating and modifying rule laws because circumstances are fluid and changing.

Modifications can come from lawmakers but also from culture. We will return to stop signs. I lived a while in Brazil. They had stop signs and rules requiring drivers to stop just as we did in the U.S. Brazilians treated stop signs differently from the way I had learned. If they came up to an intersection ahead of cars arriving from a cross street, they would honk and continue without stopping. Slowing was usually a good practice because there the stop sign had become a *de facto* yield sign. Everyone knew the procedures, including bus drivers. When I bought a car in Brazil, I adapted. Stopping at every stop sign would usually elicit stares as well as yelling and could get a person rear-ended. I ran stop signs, all the time. Was I doing wrong? No. There is no universal rule for stop signs. What works in one culture does not work in another. The U.S. way was not better than the Brazilian way or vice-versa. And before you judge, consider it likely that more than one Christian here drives over our posted speed limits.

Cultural and Individual Differences

We recognize that cultural differences affect Biblical laws also. That is why we argue over things like holy kisses or long hair. Those of us who want to cling to keeping a set of laws perfectly are forced to continually distinguish between God's absolute laws and mere cultural preferences. That gets exceedingly difficult and tedious. We might claim that God's laws never change, but we are constantly having to admit that our interpretations do migrate over the years. Things we once thought were sacred are now interpreted as cultural. I remember debates over pantsuits and kitchens in the church building. It is interesting that teachings in the Bible we interpret as cultural opinions of that time are often things we really do not want to do or do not want to change. Who wants to wash feet? Instead of trying to always judge whether some teaching is eternal or cultural, we should recognize that laws were made for our benefit and not to control us. Jesus did.

Rules laws sometimes are specific not just to cultures or countries but also to individuals. Paul explained how some Christians could eat meat offered to idols and some could not (1 Corinthians 10:14-33). A sin for me might not be a sin for you. Why is that? It is because sin is not about the rules. Rather, it is about keeping our relationship with God. I might do something that would cause me to leave the Lord but might not affect you at all. Alcohol consumption is a good example. I am personally dead set against the use and abuse of alcohol. The fact that it is legal makes no difference to me. Alcohol harms and destroys thousands of people every year, some of whom are a part of my family. I certainly cannot understand why a Christian would ever pay money for the lethal drug and support that industry. That is my opinion. Is drinking alcohol a sin for my Christian buddies? Not necessarily. Is it wrong for my Christian friend to work at a beer producer? No. Would either be a sin for me? Yes,

47

because I know those practices could lead me away from God. The point is not to get you to quit drinking alcohol, although that would be a nice side benefit. Rather, the point is for us to understand that laws and the resulting sins can be personal. You likely have things in your life that might lead to separation from God that would not affect me at all. Your rule laws and my rule laws probably differ in some respect. One set of laws does not apply to everyone.

A large problem can also develop when we start to think all laws are universal and eternal and following rules is the goal. This is particularly problematic for folks who like authority. People who profess to follow God often are law and order types. For those of us who think like that, laws are to be followed and if we follow the law, we are good. If we do not follow the law, we are bad. In our hearts, we know it is not that simple. There are people who follow the laws and rules and yet do terrible things. Likewise, there are people who do not follow all the laws and are decent people. We all believe that last sentence or we are all in trouble!

Jesus was constantly challenged by religious people concerning the law. In response, Jesus blasted them over and over. The problem was not their lack of diligence. On the contrary, the religious people were so over-zealous in following rules they missed the bigger picture. It was a huge Eureka moment when I realized that I was a lot closer to the Pharisees in the Bible than I was to the sinners! Jesus aimed a whole lot of his teachings at me, and it was not comfortable. Sometimes it was on things that seemed foreign to me like hand washing or Sabbath-keeping, but the principles he discussed were piercing. Jesus told the people they should carry the baggage of soldiers two miles even though the Roman law required only a mile (Matthew 5:41). Why? The principle is not for us to follow Roman law; the principle is to be helpful to others. The higher principle always demands more because that is the nature of God.

In John 8 we are told the teachers of the law and Pharisees brought to Jesus a woman caught in adultery. They referenced one of God's laws that she should be executed (Leviticus 20:10). You might know the end of the story: "*'Neither do I condemn you,' Jesus declared, 'Go now and leave your life of sin'*" (John 8:11 NIV). The law of God, a rule law, said the woman must die. In this case, Jesus ignored it and appealed to the principled law of mercy. We can debate that rule law all day, but we must believe that it had served a holy purpose. Jesus showed us rule laws, even those given by God, are not absolute, although principled law is. That brings us to the next question of whether God's rule laws are even necessary.

Are God's Laws Necessary?

A preacher once proclaimed at my church that for Christians there are no rules. I had to ponder that a long time since my whole life had been predicated on obeying laws. He was right in saying there is no list of rules that apply to everyone for all time and that keeping rules is not the point. However, there are always going to be rule laws to guide us and help us understand the real goals.

A friend of mine who is an elementary school teacher once told me she had only two rules in class: be kind and show respect. She then gave an example. If a child interrupts another, she reminds them that is being disrespectful. In one sense "be kind" and "show respect" are principled laws. It is easy to say those are the only two laws needed and there is some truth to that. Unfortunately, the devil is in the details. Generalities often call for more specifics. It is not enough to say, "Be respectful," as that must be explained when a child interrupts another person. A rule prohibiting interruptions will need to be created. Parents of a suspended child will not be satisfied with the explanation that their child was merely "disrespectful." They will demand specifics. In other words, we can never get away from rule laws.

When you get right down to it, rule laws are always for those who do not want to act properly in following the foundational principles such as love, mercy, and justice. Paul was aware of this when he told Timothy, "*We know that the law is good when used correctly. <u>For the law was not intended for people who do what is right.</u> It is for people who are lawless and rebellious, who are ungodly and sinful....or who do anything else that contradicts the wholesome teaching that comes from the glorious Good News entrusted to me by our blessed God*" (1 Timothy 1:8-11 NLT, Underlining added). Paul recognized that rule laws serve the same purpose in the spiritual realm as they do in the earthly realm. They point out in a specific way, primarily to the ignorant and the selfish, how to act properly. If we all acted properly, upholding the universal ideals of love, mercy, and justice, then rule laws would be unnecessary. That is why Paul explained as we move out of a life of selfishness and into a life of participation in the Spirit, we rely less and less on rule laws. He wrote, "*In the past the law held us as prisoners, but our old selves died, and we were made free from the law. So now we serve God in a* *new way, not in the old way, with the written rules. Now we serve God in the new way, with the Spirit"* (Romans 7:6 ERV). Paul understood that what he was saying would be interpreted by some to mean he wanted to do away with the law entirely. Thus a few verses later he corrected that charge by affirming, "*So then, the law is holy, and the commandment is holy, righteous and good"* (Romans 7:12 NIV).

Paul was simply saying that rule laws do not control us because the Spirit of God now controls us. We operate accordingly by making decisions, even rule law decisions, based on principled law. Rule laws can be helpful to Christians but not so absolutely. In other words, there must be an allowance for interpretation, cultural differences, individual needs, and extenuating circumstances. Certainly, rule laws are important for those who are ignorant or unaware of more noble principles and for those who choose to live apart from God. Paul recognized rule laws, though sometimes helpful, are only aids to the end goal of doing the right thing (principled law). The main point is not to follow rules; the main point is always to act according to a greater principle. Rules and laws simply point out the specific way we are to act in a given situation, if we wish to be like the Lord.

That is why all the rule laws are summed up in just two principled laws. Jesus was clear on this: "*Love the Lord your God with all your heart, soul, and mind.' This is the first and greatest commandment. The second most important is similar: 'Love your neighbor as much as you love yourself.' All the other commandments and all the demands of the prophets stem from these two laws and are fulfilled if you obey them. Keep only these and you will find that you are obeying all the others"* (Matthew 22:37-40 TLB). Paul agreed that love is the overriding principle, "*The law says, 'You must not commit adultery, you must not murder anyone, you must not steal, you must not want what belongs to someone else.' All these commands and all other commands are really only one rule: 'Love your neighbor the same as you love yourself.' Love doesn't hurt others. So loving is the same as obeying all the law*" (Romans 13:9-10 ERV). Truly, love is all we need. Laws are fine and laws are good, but even if you follow rule laws perfectly you must also follow principled law which is encapsulated in love.

We tend to think it is an either/or deal: follow principled law or follow rule laws. In the same way, we think that if we diminish rule laws in some way that we are denying their importance. That is not true. Jesus was very clear that he was not tossing out the law or its benefits. *"Do not think that I have come to abolish the Law or the Prophets; I have not come to abolish them but to fulfill them. For truly I tell you, until heaven and earth disappear, not the smallest letter, not the least stroke of a pen, will by any means disappear from the Law until everything is accomplished"* (Matthew 5:17-18 NIV). It is obvious Jesus sometimes did not follow the rule laws and gave us permission to do the same. How can Jesus say rule laws are important? It really does get down to how we approach laws and rules. Jesus was not trying to get rid of rule laws. Rather, he encourages us to put them in their place. Notice that Jesus called for fulfilling the rule laws rather than abolishing them. The idea is to complete or fill up the rules. He went on to give several specific examples of laws for which he gave a fuller interpretation. We do this by moving from a bottom-up approach to a top-down approach.

Approach to Laws

A bottom-up approach makes rule laws the king. It believes God has spoken and his laws can never be changed by humans. If the Lord makes a law, it must be eternal and irrevocable. This approach sees rule laws as absolute and binding in all situations. The laws are equal in importance and applicable in the same way to all people. Sin is defined as the breaking of laws and consequences come when sin occurs. Keeping the list of laws is how we are saved. A bottom-up approach requires all Biblical teaching to be parsed and interpreted carefully. Every teaching must be categorized as binding on us by command, binding by example, non-binding by opinion, or non-binding by culture. Christians are expected to believe alike on these interpretations.

On the other hand, a top-down approach recognizes that rule laws can be good and helpful. However, this approach says rule laws are always secondary to the principled laws of love, mercy, justice, kindness, patience, etc. Every action, including following rule laws, must be interpreted by principled law.

Taking a top-down approach has many benefits over the commonly held bottom-up approach. For one, it ends a great deal of perceived guilt among Christians. Real guilt, of course, arises from sin or other wrongdoing. However, perceived guilt can cause many of the same symptoms of stress and depression as the real variety. I believe much of our felt guilt comes from our perception we must follow all laws, something we cannot do. Thirty-one percent of churchgoers in a recent survey selected "obligation" as one of the reasons for their attendance. Next time you are in church services look to the person on your left and then to the one on your right. That means one of you is there at least partly out of a sense of trying to follow the laws!

Two, a top-down approach helps us make better decisions in our lives. The other approach leans heavily on following the law no matter the hurt that otherwise might cause. Mercy and love can easily be overlooked under the righteous disguise of a need to be law-abiding. When there is a real or perceived conflict between the two laws, principled law should be followed. God said, "*I want you to show love, not offer sacrifices. I want you to know me more than I want burnt offerings*" (Hosea 6:6 NLT). God acknowledged the better choice in this passage. Rule laws can be modified when they disregard principled law. No one is advocating anarchy, but love and mercy should be the drivers as we write, interpret, and apply laws in all parts of our life. Doing so will make our decisions much better and will mitigate a lot of mistakes. As Peter conveyed, "*Above all, love each other deeply, because love covers over a multitude of sins*" (1 Peter 4:8 NIV). If we are going to err, we should err in favor of principled law.

Three, choosing the better approach widens our circle. Tolerance is often seen as a dirty word by religious people in general because it implies some sort of deviation from the standard. The requirement that everyone adheres to a particular list of laws is precisely what Jesus so roundly condemned. "*Woe to you, teachers of the law and Pharisees, you hypocrites! You shut the door of the kingdom of heaven in people's faces. Yourselves do not enter, nor will you let those enter who are trying to. Woe to you, teachers of the law and Pharisees, you hypocrites! You travel over land and* sea to win a single convert, and when you have succeeded, you make them twice as much a child of hell as you are" (Matthew 23:13, 15 NIV). What exactly were the teachers of the laws and the Pharisees doing that made Jesus so angry? They had made a list of what they considered to be God's laws and demanded people follow that list. How is it different when we do the same thing?

Four, the top-down approach holds us to a higher standard. The accusation is always that such an approach encourages people to go hog-wild and do whatever they want. The reality is that relying primarily on principled law constantly calls us to go the extra mile, turn the other cheek, refuse to sue each other, and give abundantly. When mere love becomes sacrificial, unconditional, and steadfast it morphs into the love of God. "*We love because he first loved us*" (1 John 4:19 NIV).

Final thoughts on Rules and Laws

Rule laws will always be with us and can be very useful. Keep in mind a few things about them:

- They do change from time to time and there is a certain amount of relativity in them. No one believes all laws are absolute for all times and all situations. Walking in the street is one example, but even things like killing come to mind. Is all killing bad? What about self-defense, birth control, abortion, euthanasia, war, or capital punishment? All these things have been debated by the world and by the church.

- They are imperfect. They cannot cover all circumstances. People keep finding ways to get around rules and to interpret rules differently and to our own advantage.
- There is no end to laws. The Bible does not even have every rule listed. It lists some things that we do not believe are sins and there are some sins it does not list.
- We endlessly debate and argue over laws. We each create our own list of laws. I can almost guarantee that my list is different somewhat from yours.
- We apply laws differently to ourselves than we do to others. That can add the element of emotion which leads to inconsistencies. An old saying is: "Don't tax me. Don't tax thee. Tax the man behind the tree."
- Laws become the goal and not the means to the goal. If we do not follow the principled law of love for God and neighbor, then it does not matter how well we follow any rule laws.

4 Are Christians Really Sinners?

> Jane Aubrey, on the first date with a star pitcher, although she knew very little about baseball: "Do you lose very much?"
>
> Billy Chapel: "I lose. I've lost 134 times."
>
> Aubrey: "You count them?"
>
> Chapel: "We count everything."
>
> (*For the Love of the Game*, Dir: Sam Raimi, Universal Pictures, 1999)

IT IS EASY FOR US TO TIE A SPECIFIC SIN to the breaking of a specific law, one of the rule laws usually found in the Bible or accepted widely in the Church as a rule law. In that view, breaking a law is sin and there is no sin when no law is broken. John showed a connection between sin and the breaking of law when he stated "*Anyone who sins breaks God's law. Yes, sinning is the same as living against God's law*" (1 John 3:4 ERV).

As simple as we would like that to be, there are several problems in associating sin only with the breaking of rule laws. As already mentioned, rule laws in and of themselves have limitations. Their only importance comes when they point to the greater danger that leads to our separation from God.

Jesus recognized this when he noted the insufficiency of law not backed up by the greater principle. He assured the original followers of the Law that *"until heaven and earth disappear, not even the smallest detail of God's law will disappear until its purpose is achieved"* (Matthew 5:18 NLT). He went on with a few examples of how sin really has to do with ignoring the main principles rather than the breaking of a named law.

In the first of these, he said, *"You have heard the commandment that says, 'You must not commit adultery. But I say, anyone who even looks at a woman with lust has already committed adultery with her in his heart"* (Matthew 5:27-28 NLT). The prohibition against adultery finds its meaning in the overarching goals of people treating others respectfully and of faithfulness in marriage. Adultery is a sin not just because there is a specific rule law but also because adultery creates mistrust, hurts individuals, and destroys families. Looking to the wider perspective, as Jesus did, demands even more from us.

Jesus later referenced another rule law, by referring to a Biblical law commanding tithing, *"You're hopeless, you religion scholars and Pharisees! Frauds! You keep meticulous account books, tithing on every nickel and dime you get, but on the meat of God's Law, things like fairness and compassion and commitment—the absolute basics! —you carelessly take it or leave it. Careful bookkeeping is commendable, but the basics are required. Do you have any idea how silly you look, writing a life story that's wrong from start to finish, nitpicking over commas and semicolons"* (Matthew 23:23-24 MSG)? Jesus was not disputing or negating the tithing law. Measured giving demonstrates divine qualities such as fairness, compassion, and commitment so tithing was designated a rule law under Moses. Failure to tithe became sin whenever tithing was decoupled from its underlying goal and not simply because a rule was neglected.

From these teachings of Jesus, we reinforce the idea that sin is not defined just by breaking the law. Sin's real danger occurs whenever sin leads us to be separated from God. That is because being in sin or being sinful means being away from the Lord. The inverse is also true. Being with God means we are not in sin and are not sinful. That brings up the inevitable dilemma. Although Christians are characterized as not in sin, we do break the law and we do things noted as sins in the Bible. How do we reconcile these realities?

Free from Sin

We will begin by going back to the earlier metaphor of life and death. As you recall, to be in Christ is to live and to be away from Christ is to die. This is not referring to our physical lives and deaths, although our earthly death does seem to have some roots in sin. Rather, life and death refer to our relationship with God or lack thereof. Death comes because of sin. James put it this way: "*You are tempted by the evil things you want. Your own desire leads you away and traps you. Your desire grows inside you until it results in sin. Then the sin grows bigger and bigger and finally ends in death*" (James 1:14-15 ERV). James laid out for us the common progression from temptation to sin and eventually to death. Interestingly, he did not say that all sin leads to death. In other words, not all sin results in separation from God. John made this even plainer when he wrote, "*There is sin that leads to death. Doing wrong is always sin. But there is sin that does not lead to eternal death*" (1 John 5:16-17 ERV).

Realizing that the Bible talks of sin in two different ways helps us understand John's next assertion, "*We know that whoever is born of God does not sin; but he who has been born of God keeps himself, and the wicked one does not touch him*" (1 John 5:18 NKJV). John acknowledged that for Christians there is some sin that leads to death and there is some sin that does not (1 John 5:16-17). Christians do commit sins and break laws. How then could John say we do not sin or cannot continue sinning? When he proclaimed there is no sin in us when we are in Christ, he was saying that Christians are not in the state of sin or in the state of separation from God. We cannot be in sin and in Christ at the same time. We cannot be in and out. We might commit a sin, but such sin does not necessarily result in death. John affirmed we cannot indulge in sin that separates us from God while we are Christians.

This may not be what you were taught. I grew up hearing all sin is equally bad and that committing even one sin will always separate us from God. I have even been known to teach that although it is not taught in the Bible. One sin can conceivably be the vehicle that carries us away from the Lord. However, the Scriptures do not teach that every sin every time causes us to be separated from God. We cannot disregard the intent of the person, forgiveness by God, the extent of harm caused, and other factors.

Separation from God results from our choice to live a sinful life away from God as opposed to not living with him in the way he created us. It does not result from a single sin or the single breaking of a rule, Adam and Eve notwithstanding. When they sank their teeth into the fruit it was not a casual moment of weakness. Instead, they were making a choice to live the way they wanted to and not in the way God intended. They wanted to be God and to be free from God. "*The serpent told the Woman, 'You won't die. God knows that the moment you eat from that tree, you'll see what's really going on. <u>You'll be just like God, knowing everything</u>, ranging all the way from good to evil.' When the Woman saw that the tree looked like good eating <u>and realized what she would get out of it—she'd know everything!</u>—she took and ate the fruit and then gave some to her husband, and he ate*" (Genesis 3:4-6 MSG, Underlining added). Eating the fruit was not the point at all just as committing a single sin is never the point. The point of sin and what makes it potentially fatal is our choosing a life separated from God. Sin can and does lead to spiritual death.

Even a single sin, which may seem tame, will be a concern because any sin can lead a person to rebellion from God. Since no one likes the horrible consequences of sin, the obvious solution would be to stay away from sin entirely. As we all know, that is not as simple as it may sound. People sometimes look for other solutions. For non-Christians, that solution is most often the complete denial of sins altogether. If there are no sins, the thinking goes, then there can be neither punishment nor guilt coming from the commission of a sin. It is hard to consistently keep this position. We know that because almost everyone appeals to moral standards and recognizes the opposite of those standards. Most humans recognize good and bad behavior and feel the consequences of their actions. Another common solution to dealing with sin is to redefine it. Sin then is not defined in terms of our relationship with God. Instead, it is reimagined as some form of vice or lack of self-control. Thus, we talk of the sinful pleasures of too much chocolate or the social *faux pas* of breaking some politically correct norm. Christians cannot turn to denials or different definitions. For us, sin is a real danger that can never be minimized.

When we commit a sin, while a Christian or before we became a Christian, we are breaking some law, either principled law or both rule laws and principled law. However, for sin to lead to death, it must be a part of our checking the not God box. That choice can be a verbal expression or stated confession. There are people who publicly or privately deny and denounce God or Jesus Christ. The choice can also be made by our actions, the way we choose to live our life. Paul reminded us, *"Follow God's example in everything you do just as a much-loved child imitates his father. Be full of love for others, following the example of Christ who loved you and gave himself to God as a sacrifice to take away your sins"* (Ephesians 5:1-2 TLB). Choosing God means a changed life, lived as though we are in his image. A person who chooses to live a life of sin apart from the Lord will be living in sin and not in Christ, whether they openly deny God or not. On the other hand, it could be argued any choice of a life of sin is a denial of the power of God.

The Effect of Sin

Let me reiterate that committing a sin does not always lead to the state of sin (James 1:14-15, 1 John 5:16-17). Sin is a mortal wound when it is part of our choice to leave God or prevents us from serving God. All sins are potentially dangerous and are to be avoided. Nonetheless, not all sins are fatal. I will use drugs as an example. A single injection can cause death. We know that. We also know there are many cases where a single dose causes neither death nor addiction. Is it okay to shoot up once? Opinions might vary, but most people would agree a single dose is potentially dangerous. Paul applied some of this thinking to sin in 1 Corinthians 6. Beginning in verse 9, he contrasted the unrighteous who will not inherit the kingdom of God with Christians who have been washed, sanctified, and justified through Jesus Christ and the Spirit. What separated these two groups? The unrighteous were living in a state of sin. Sin is a general word and often requires specifics, so Paul gave us the specific categories with his partial list. *"Neither the sexually immoral, nor idolaters, nor adulterers, nor men who practice homosexuality, nor thieves, nor the greedy, nor drunkards, nor revilers, nor swindlers will inherit the kingdom of God"* (1 Corinthians 6:9-10 ESV). It would be easy to interpret Paul as saying that whoever commits a theft or an immoral sexual act is unrighteous. He did not make that claim. He could have. Instead, he said the unrighteousness resulted from those who were in the general state of sin and the specific state of greed, drunkenness, swindling, etc. Those people were apart from God because their continued indulgence in sinful acts kept them from participating in the holiness of the Lord.

To say a Christian is not sinful is to confirm they are free from sin. What does it mean to be free of sin? We can ask a similar question. What does it mean to be free of disease? People who are free of disease currently do not have a disease. They may have had some disease in the past and may catch it in the future, but currently, they are without the disease. They are not in a state of illness. The disease has no power over them and is not affecting them. It is untrue and unfair to say they still have a disease because they once had it. They may currently have bacteria and viruses living in them yet have no sickness. In the same way, any Christian who is freed from sin has no sin and is not in sin. Sin has no power over anyone in Christ. A Christian might be exposed to sin by breaking God's laws and committing sins but still not be sinful or in sin. A person in Christ is not at the same time in sin. A Christian is free from sin and the deadly effects of sin. If we are born of God or saved, we are living in Jesus Christ and not living in sin. We cannot be in light and darkness (not light) at the same time. We cannot be in life and death (not-life) at the same time. We cannot be in God and be in sin (not God) at the same time.

I would like to give another example of how this works. When I was young my dad had a vegetable garden. He grew many things, but his greatest success was okra. He was a prolific producer, supplying not only us but others as well. In season, he wanted me to pick the okra daily. Okra comes with tiny but itchy hairs, and I did not like the job. My dad reasoned I spent most of my time watching TV and therefore 15 minutes a day was not too much for a kid to contribute to the family. I reasoned since I did not like the taste of okra, I should not have to be the one to do the picking. So much for my dad issues. For the garden to be successful, it had to be maintained. Weeds were constantly sprouting and, if left unattended, could take over the garden and render it useless.

On more than one occasion Jesus used weeds as metaphors so I feel safe in doing the same. Sins are like weeds in our vegetable gardens. They are constantly popping up no matter what one does to prevent them. If they are eliminated through hoeing or chemicals, no damage is done. Weeds can destroy the garden, but not every weed does. If you had ventured into my back yard, you would have seen my dad's vegetable garden. You would not have seen a weed bed, nor would you have called it such. You would have complimented him on the fine vegetable garden even though there was a variety of weeds sprouting daily. The presence of a few weeds did not cause the nature of the garden to change. It was a wonderful garden producing lovely vegetables. In no sense was it controlled by weeds or in the state of weeds. We can say the garden was weed-free because it was being tended to and no weeds could harm the vegetables or change the vegetable garden to a weed garden. In the same way, we can be counted as sin-free even though sometimes sins are committed.

I do not want to minimize sin in any way. Sin is extremely dangerous because sin can lead to death. Any sin can be lethal, but not all sins go that far. Just as small weeds can grow to destroy the garden, sin can destroy us. Any person can choose to be apart from the Lord either by the overt choice of denial or by the less direct choice of engaging in a life of activities that are not God-like. Christians are not immune from making those regrettable life choices. It may be uncommon for Christians to abandon the freedom of the Spirit and to return to the slavery of sin. It can and does happen. We are warned of shifting allegiances (Colossians 1:21-23, Hebrews 10:23-31).

Probably the most graphic warning came from Peter: "*For if, after they have escaped the defilements of the world through the knowledge of our Lord and Savior Jesus Christ, they are again entangled in them and overcome, the last state has become worse for them than the first. For it would have been better for them never to have known the way of righteousness than after knowing it to turn back from the holy commandment delivered to them. What the true proverb says has happened to them: 'The dog returns to its own vomit, and the sow, after washing herself, returns to wallow in the mire'*" (2 Peter 2:20-22 ESV). As bad as that may sound, separation only happens when Christians choose to turn away from God. Notice Peter was not referencing the commitment of a single sin. Rather, the problem was people who turned away and who became overcome with a life of sin. If we remain in God and let him tend our garden, then we can have a beautiful life free from sin.

No Longer a Sinner

If we are in Christ and not in sin, it seems to follow we also are not sinners. That conclusion might not come easily for some Christians. It did not for me. Christians commonly accept we are blameless, free from sin, and even not in sin, yet balk at saying we are therefore not sinners. We will look at why we claim Christians are not sinners.

4 Are Christians Really Sinners?

It makes sense to tie the definition of a sinner to the meaning of sin. Sin is connected to rebellion. That rebellion, without forgiveness, leads to permanent separation from God. Logically, if sin is the choice to separate from God, then a sinner is one who has chosen to be separated from God. We have stressed that Christians are not in sin and not sinful. Therefore, we can extrapolate that Christians are also not sinners. To be in sin is to be apart from the Lord. In the same way, a sinner is one who is not with God.

While succinct, this causes some concern. Whenever we present the idea Christians are not sinners, someone will invariably raise questions: "Don't we still commit sins even after baptism?" and "Doesn't that mean we are still sinners?" The underlying assumption is that committing even one sin makes us a sinner. People who take this position might refer to the common dictionary definition that a sinner is one who sins. While that makes some sense, it does not tell the whole story. For example, I do not consider myself a builder. I have built birdhouses and shelves, but those activities do not make me a builder. If you wanted to remodel your den, you would not consult with me! You would call a builder. Building an item does not necessarily make me a builder. Committing a sin does not necessarily make me a sinner.

Definitions can bring up problems. Some Christians define sinner one way, and some define it a different way. The different definitions of sinner usually are tied to the different ways we define sin. If sin is defined only as the breaking of a rule, then it is natural to define a sinner as one who has broken a rule. In that view, we have all broken at least one rule and thus have sinned so we must eternally remain a sinner. There are several problems with this narrow thinking about sin and being a sinner. One, defining sin in this way focuses on the action of sin rather than considering the effect of sin as well. As noted, sin's danger comes from the results of sin and not the mere act. Two, saying sin is only breaking a law leads to the conclusion all humans are sinners their entire life. Such a definition then is useless because the word sinner simply becomes a synonym for the word human. Three, labeling a person a sinner for life due to the commission of just one sin denies the power of God to change our very nature. When we enter Jesus Christ, our whole being is changed. We are radically different from what we used to be. It is unhelpful and, I believe, untrue to say a person must carry the burden of being a sinner based on having, at some point, committed a sin.

A Sinner is in Sin

On the other hand, if the sin definition includes the intention or choice of moving from God as well as the breaking of rules, then the definition of a sinner must also include a person's current choice of God or not God. This seems to be the more logical approach we can learn from the Word. The Bible does not give us a dictionary definition of a sinner. Because of that, we must see how the Bible understands the sinner rather than relying solely on our popular conceptions. In the Scriptures, a sinner is often associated with wickedness (Psalm 1:1,5; 37:8). A sinner is not righteous. He or she has not chosen God and is not in a relationship with God. The righteousness which is found in Yahweh contrasts sharply with the wickedness of the sinner

(Proverbs 13:6, 21). Therefore, the sinner is identified as godless and in rebellion, destined for punishment (Isaiah 1:28; 13:9; 33:14; Psalm 104:35). Ezekiel summarized this understanding: "*If a righteous person turns to sinning and acts like any other sinner, should he be allowed to live? No, of course not. All his previous goodness will be forgotten and he shall die for his sins*" (Ezekiel 18:24 TLB). Ezekiel made the distinction between being a righteous person and being a sinner. Righteous people are involved in righteous behavior and sinners in sinful behavior. They have chosen different paths.

Paul took the idea a step further by showing how being a sinner was part of our earlier life and being righteous is associated with our current Christian life: "*You see, at just the right time, when we were still powerless, Christ died for the ungodly. Very rarely will anyone die for a righteous person, though for a good person someone might possibly dare to die. But God demonstrates his own love for us in this: While we were still sinners, Christ died for us. Since we have now been justified by his blood, how much more shall we be saved from God's wrath through him! For if, while we were God's enemies, we were reconciled to him through the death of his Son, how much more, having been reconciled, shall we be saved through his life! Not only is this so, but we also boast in God through our Lord Jesus Christ, through whom we have now received reconciliation*" (Romans 5:6-11 NIV). Paul said there was a time in our lives when we were powerless, enemies of God, ungodly, and, yes, sinners. Those related words all describe the former life of sin and estrangement. That all changed when Christ died for us, and we accepted that life. Paul was clear we were once enemies but are now reconciled and saved through the death of the Son (verse 10). He was equally clear in the parallel verse we were once sinners but are now justified and saved through that death (verse 9). The Redeemer brought his saving power to us when we were sinners and not when we were righteous. Now we are justified. Now we are saved. Now we are reconciled to the Father. We are no longer ungodly or enemies. Equally important, we are no longer sinners.

Jesus verified this either/or contrast when he declared, "*I have not come to call the righteous, but sinners to repentance*" (Luke 5:32 NIV). In the verse prior to this, he refers to himself as a doctor who helped the sick instead of aiding people who are already well. He delineated two groups of people, healthy people (the righteous) and sick people (sinners). These groups stand for those who had chosen God and those who have rejected God. Plainly, Jesus wanted to transform sinners into the righteous through repentance. Repentance signifies a true life change so that we become something different. Jesus did not, as some imagine, see a group of righteous sinners and a group of unrighteous sinners. Why is that distinction important? It is commonly accepted among Christians today that we all continue to be sinners despite being righteous with God. Jesus was clear not everyone is a sinner. There are the righteous and there are sinners. He showed us that people are sinners before they become righteous and that when they are righteous, they are no longer sinners. The goal is to move them from being sinners to being righteous. This is vastly different from prevalent Christian thought that claims when sinners are saved, they become saved sinners. Sinners do not become sinners (saved or otherwise) and the saved do not remain sinners. When saved, sinners move out of sin and into Jesus Christ. They go from being sick to being well. *"Once you were dead because of your disobedience and your many sins. You used to live in sin, just like the rest of the world, obeying the devil—the commander of the powers in the unseen world. He is the spirit at work in the hearts of those who refuse to obey God. All of us used to live that way, following the passionate desires and inclinations of our sinful nature. By our very nature we were subject to God's anger, just like everyone else. But God is so rich in mercy, and he loved us so much, that even though we were dead because of our sins, he gave us life when he raised Christ from the dead. (It is only by God's grace that you have been saved)"* (Ephesians 2:1-5 NLT)!

Why does the belief persist among Christians that we still are sinners, although we are saved from sin? Why do saints all know we are not ungodly and are not enemies of the King yet have a hard time believing we are no longer sinners? There are several reasons. One reason is that we still want to limit our definition of sin to something like breaking a rule, not being perfect, or not doing enough good deeds. The thinking goes that since Christians do sometimes break laws, are not perfect, and could do more good deeds then we must be sinners. We have tried to show that this narrow definition is not Biblical. It only serves to produce in us a lot of felt guilt. While sin has some elements of law-breaking or imperfection, it must be defined in the broader context of our choices. Therefore, a sinner must be one who has chosen to be outside of Christ.

Another reason is that traditionally we were taught humans are made up of a spiritual component and a bodily component. The bodily portion is sometimes called our sinful nature or flesh. Some theologians believe that we are born with this sinful nature and will never be able to escape it fully until the spiritual portion separates and leaves behind the bodily portion. This is a reason some cannot give up the idea that we remain sinners, even after we enter redemption. Without going into too much detail, suffice it to say this idea is faulty because it denies the power of the blood to save the whole person. Paul concurred, "*You have stripped off your old sinful nature and all its wicked deeds. Put on your new nature, and be renewed as you learn to know your Creator and become like him*" (Colossians 3:9-10 NLT).

A third reason saints have a hard time believing we are no longer sinners is that many Christians think we will appear arrogant to outsiders if we claim we are not sinners. That is because we still equate being a sinner with being imperfect. Christians are hesitant to say we are perfect so feel it necessary to admit we are still sinners.

I understand why the idea that Christians are sinners has flourished, but I also recognize we need to look at how the Bible views a sinner and not how we commonly do. In the Bible, Christians are no longer sinners. It is troubling many believers still view themselves that way. Why is that a problem? Quite simply, identifying as a sinner is essentially denying the needle has moved for Christians. It is severely limiting God's ability to transform us. It is admitting defeat and acquiescing to the power of evil. It is diluting our message because we are not able to lay out a case for our hope. What appeal do we have to a sinful world when we have a hard time distinguishing between life in sin and life in Christ? I dare not speak for others, but I can confidently proclaim I am not a sinner. That confidence has nothing to do with me and everything to do with the saving power of the Son. I am free from sin, the power of sin, and the consequences of sin. Sin has no power over me and cannot separate me from the Lord unless I should unfathomably choose to walk away from him.

Do Christians Struggle with Sin?

Within the last two weeks, once from my preacher and once from a class member at a different church, I heard that all Christians sin daily. The idea that all people, saved and unsaved alike, sin daily or continuously is a common belief among Christians. Perhaps the idea is simply connected to the prevailing thought that Christians are still sinners. Some see sin as so prevalent it must be perpetually unavoidable. Certainly, this belief in the inevitability of sin leads us to the conclusion that we must battle constantly with sin. As noted earlier, anyone who defends this position invariably turns to Paul.

We need to revisit the passage in Romans 7 where Paul discussed a struggle with sin. It is important that we deal with this passage because so many Christians cite it as normative for each of us. "*I know that nothing good lives in me, that is, in my sinful nature. I want to do what is right, but I can't. I want to do what is good, but I don't. I don't want to do what is wrong, but I do it anyway. But if I do what I don't want to do, I am not really the one doing wrong; it is sin living in me that does it*" (Romans 7:18-20 NLT).

Although written in the present tense, the context suggests Paul used a literary device to emphasize the power sin had in his former not God state. The struggle with sin was not happening during Paul's present time as a Christian. It described his life when he was not a Christian. He was not saying that Christians struggle in sin while they are Christians. In fact, he indicated the opposite. In the preceding chapter, Paul wrote "*We know that our old sinful selves were crucified with Christ. We are no longer slaves to sin. For when we died with Christ we were set free from the power of sin*" (Romans 6:6-7 NLT). He made the same contrast between God and not God by using the terms of freedom/slavery.

How was Paul able to say his sinful self is dead, he was not a slave to sin, he was free from sin, and yet said he is struggling with sin? He did not. He talked of one state as the condition in which he was a slave to sin. While struggling with sin, he was in the sinful state. "*I really want to obey God's law, but because of my sinful nature I am a slave to sin*" (Romans 7:25 NLT). That was then. Now is different. When we die with Christ we move out of that state where sin has power and into the state of freedom from sin. Paul reiterated this by contrasting the *then* life as living in the passion of sin but the *now* life as living in the Spirit. "*<u>In the past</u> we were ruled by our sinful selves....So <u>now</u> we serve God in a new way, not in the old way, with the written rules. <u>Now</u> we serve God in the new way, with the Spirit*" (Romans 7:5-6 ERV, Underlining added). Earlier in our lives, we were controlled by the sinful nature and were slaves to sin. Now, the Spirit controls us, and we are free from sins. There is no way Paul intended to say Christians are now controlled by sin.

I understand that some interpreters will reject my opinions and still say Paul was referring to a struggle with sin during his Christian life. In one sense, proving or disproving what Paul intended does not help us. Why? Even if we prove Paul was not saying he struggled with sin as a Christian that does not disprove that you or I might do so. In fact, I have had fellow Christians tell me that Paul's words must have been about his Christian life because those very words echo their own experience! Certainly, it is a prevailing thought among Christians that we do struggle constantly with sin. My problem is reconciling that belief with the equally strong belief that as Christians we are not sinful, we are not living in sin, and we are not sinners. I want to examine this idea of a struggle some more.

What Does it Mean to Struggle?

Putting aside the "when" of Paul's struggle, focus on the struggle itself. The core of his struggle was this: "*I want to do what is good, but I don't. I don't want to do what is wrong, but I do it anyway*" (Romans 7:19 NLT). As Christians, we also want to do good, and we want to please God and others. It is our nature. Yet, we make mistakes, and we commit sins. This gap between our desires and reality seems to set up a struggle.

A struggle can be defined as contending with a force or enemy. Paul described this adversary as the sin living in him. What did he mean by that? He wanted to make the right choices. His description of the struggle was about decision making. That included the choice to do good and the choice to avoid the bad. We have said that sin involves choice. Sins we commit do not keep us from our Savior because we have chosen him, and he has chosen us. Consider such classic examples as Peter, Abraham, and David. They engaged in lying, denying the Lord, adultery, and murder. By many accounts, those sins might seem to make them anathema to God. In contrast to human judgment, all of them were held up as honorable leaders by the Lord. Why? They continued to choose God despite the sins they committed during that relationship.

In these verses, Paul explained that sin was preventing him from reaching the desired goal of being with God. He was not referring to sins he might commit as a Christian but the kind of elected sin state that kept him apart from his Maker. Is sin an outside force or evil that prevented him from doing right? No, sin was the result of his choices. Despite claiming "the Devil made me do it," we must acknowledge any sin that affects us must originate from within us. Satan may have the power to deceive and influence our decisions, but sin is essentially internal. Any struggle, therefore, results from our not making the right choice 100% of the time. Paul classically described the struggle in terms of trying to be righteous with God. For him, the struggle was about trying to be perfect through the process of making perfect decisions. Paul's battle was tied to the need for keeping the law perfectly and earning his salvation. That is why he equated freedom from sin as being free from following every rule (Romans 7:6). He clarified, "*Sin is no longer your master, for you no longer live under the requirements of the law*" (Romans 6:14 NLT).

Like Paul, we realize that perfection on our own is impossible for us. Hence, a struggle can take place for all people. However, Christians do not have that struggle anymore. We have made the choice of God, so we do not need to keep making that choice over and over. Also, we do not have a constant struggle with sin because we do not need to be perfect. We have been set free from the law of sin and death. We are free from trying to keep every rule. We are not struggling with having to be perfect as Paul and many of us have done before.

I certainly understand why the world struggles with sin. Sin controls and enslaves, cutting people off from their Creator. However, I do not fully understand why we are taught that all Christians also constantly struggle with sin. When one is free from sin and sin has no power to do harm then how is it Christians feel a struggle with sin? I believe it is because we are more concerned with our imperfections than we are with grace. We feel God expects more from us and we continue trying to please and improve to gain God's favor. Obviously, Christians still commit sins, still break the rules, and still make bad choices. Doesn't that mean we are in a struggle to not sin? No! We may commit sins, but we are not going through the battle with living in sin that Paul described when he was struggling to be righteous. Like Paul, we no longer have that struggle when we enter the Spirit. We are not living in sin and still trying to conquer sin. We are victorious and will be victorious through Jesus Christ. The idea of a struggle implies there is a battle we might lose. Struggle means we still think we are failing or might be failing. Struggle shows we feel guilt and inadequacies. Struggle suggests we are in the waters and not in the lifeboat. None of this applies to our life in Jesus Christ. Christians are not losing. We are not failing. We are not battling. We are not guilty.

Yet, we still want to flounder around in the waves. Some of us believe we are in the same struggle with sin we had before joining the ranks of the saints. I dare not condemn a sincere Christian who claims to be battling with sin still. It does happen as some Christians struggle with their choice to stay with God. Some might battle with the kind of sin that can lead them from God. Most Christians, on the other hand, do not fight with a constant desire or inclination to leave the Lord. I contend it is not normal for Christians to struggle with sin. We know there are tons of great marriages and other relationships that do not involve a continuing struggle with keeping them together. The fact that some relationships end badly and the fact that many relationships might meet occasional bumps does not mean all relationships involve constant daily struggles.

We might struggle with trying to be perfect or not break any laws, but we do not need to battle constantly with sins that might be fatal. Those sins tied to imperfections or breaking laws are overcome in Jesus Christ and do not lead to death. My point is that Christians live in far too much fear of committing a sin. We think too much about sin and too little about the Spirit. Sin can be extremely dangerous in the context of our choosing a sinful life over a Spirit-filled life. In that respect, I do not in any way want to discount the power of sin. Rather, I want to emphasize the power of the blood. It is much bigger and more dynamic than any sins we might commit as Christians. *"My dear children, I am writing this to you so you will not sin. But if anyone does sin, there is One*

Who will go between him and the Father. He is Jesus Christ, the One Who is right with God. He paid for our sins with His own blood. He did not pay for ours only, but for the sins of the whole world" (1 John 2:1-2 NLT). Temptations to do wrong will arise and we sometimes give in to the temptations, but such sins are being defeated and do not keep us from the Lord.

This whole section of Romans 7-8 was never intended to be a dark assessment of a Christian life mired in sin, producing a never-ending stream of fear and anxiety. Rather, it is a celebration of our new life that does not include any struggle with keeping count of all our sins. Paul summarized it well: "*Who shall separate us from the love of Christ? Shall trouble or hardship or persecution or famine or nakedness or danger or sword...In all these things we are more than conquerors through him who loved us. For I am convinced that neither death nor life, neither angels nor demons, neither the present nor the future, nor any powers, neither height nor depth, nor anything else in all creation, will be able to separate us from the love of God that is in Christ Jesus our Lord*" (Romans 8:35. 37-39 NIV). How can we believe those words and still believe we are all in a continuing struggle with sin? In the next few chapters, we want to discuss the process that makes the question unnecessary.

5 Can God Forgive That Sin?

> Pete Hogwallop: "Delmar's been saved."
>
> Delmar O'Donnel: "That's it, boys. I've been redeemed. The preacher's done washed away all my sins and transgressions. It's the straight and narrow from here on out. And heaven everlasting is my reward. The preacher said all my sins is washed away, including that Piggly Wiggly I knocked over in Yazoo."
>
> Ulysses Everett McGill: "I thought you said you were innocent of those charges."
>
> O'Donnel: "Well, I was lying, and the preacher said that that sin's been washed away too. Neither God nor man has nothing on me now. Come on in. The water is fine."
>
> (*O Brother, Where Art Thou?* Dir: Joel Cohen, Buena Vista Pictures Distribution and Universal Pictures, 2000)

FIRST GRADE WAS TRAUMATIC FOR ME. I did not attend kindergarten and had not been away from home by myself that much. Naturally, on the first day of school, I was a little heartbroken and did shed a few tears. It helped that my teacher seemed to be empathetic. On the second day of school, Mrs. Carter came full of optimism that lifted my spirits. Then she elaborated the reason for her excitement. "Children," she exclaimed to the entire class, "we had a wonderful first day. Only one boy cried!" When I looked up, it seemed nineteen sets of eyes aimed at me like daggers.

First grade improved and my confidence grew until we received our first report card. On the bus home, I sat by my next-door neighbor, a worldly-wise third grader named Junior. I trusted him since he had helped me earlier in the year by getting me on the right bus. Junior asked to see my report card and I obliged. He looked at it briefly, shook his head slowly and asked if I knew what it meant. I did not, so he enlightened me: "It is not very good. All of these S's mean sorry. You have straight *Sorrys*." The first day had taught me not to cry in public, but after exiting the bus I let out a stream of tears. Fortunately, my always-understanding mom reassured me that I did not have a plethora of *Sorrys*. Indeed, the S's were straight *Satisfactorys*! My point? Many of us in the church still live under a fair amount of guilt feelings and insecurity because we have had the Juniors of the church telling us we are sorry when, in fact, God has pronounced us very satisfactory. To understand why, we will present a couple of basic principles that come into play because of Christ. These are foundational arguments. I need for you to completely understand and agree with them. Both tenets seem rather simple and uncomplicated so it would be easy to nod acceptance. If you are a follower of Jesus Christ, you certainly think you do believe. Note there is *belief* and there is *BELIEF*. I want you to really believe these two key points because the implications for your life can be staggering. If I cannot get you onboard for both ideas, then be assured that the rest of the book will be a waste of time.

Everything?

The first tenet is this: when God forgives your sin, he forgives ALL your sins. There is no partial forgiveness. God does not pick and choose. He does not hold back. As John encouraged, "*We should live in the light, where God is. If we live in the light, we have fellowship with each other, and the blood sacrifice of Jesus, God's Son, washes away every sin and makes us clean*" (1 John 1:7 ERV).

John was not the only one who made the point God takes away all our sins through Jesus. In the Bible, things said only one time get us all worked up. Take, for example, the fact that Paul mentioned baptism for the dead (1 Corinthians 15:29). He did so only once and without a lot of explanation, so we endlessly debate and guess what this might mean. Conversely, when a subject is talked about repeatedly in the Scriptures, we must pay even more attention. The idea that forgiveness is for all our sins is found everywhere in the Bible. For example:

- "*You forgave the guilt of your people— yes, you covered all their sins*" (Psalm 85:2 NLT).
- "*He forgives all my sins and heals all my diseases*" (Psalm 103:3 NLT).
- "*Repent therefore, and turn back, that your sins may be blotted out*" (Acts 3:19 ESV).
- "*I will forgive their wickedness, and I will never again remember their sins*" (Hebrews 8:12; Jeremiah 31:34 NLT).
- "*You were dead in sins, and your sinful desires were not yet cut away. Then he gave you a share in the*

> very life of Christ, for he forgave all your sins, and blotted out the charges proved against you, the list of his commandments which you had not obeyed. He took this list of sins and destroyed it by nailing it to Christ's cross" (Colossians 2:13-15 TLB).

We know all our sins are forgiven by God, but often we have not completely absorbed the full implications. Allow me to try a little math. If I have a bucket of balls and I take away ALL the balls, how many are left in the bucket? The answer is zero, of course. There are no balls left if I take all of them away. What if we began with 10 balls in the bucket and I remove all of them? None left. 100 balls? The same. None left. 10,000 balls? Still, none left. No matter how many balls began in the bucket, no balls are left in the bucket after they are all removed. When God forgives, he forgives completely. When he takes away all your sins, there are no sins left in you. Nada. It must be that way because even leaving one ball behind means we have not removed all of them.

God's Love vs. Our Love

One of the most iconic images of God is that of a parent. Most often he is referred to as a father but also as a mother. Jesus employs the metaphor of family as a powerful image of the love God has for us. He used a common rabbinic argument style called a much-more argument when he questioned: "*Which of you fathers, if your son asks for a fish, will give him a snake instead? Or if he asks for an egg, will give him a scorpion? If you then, though you are evil, know how to give good gifts to your children, how much more will your Father in heaven give the Holy Spirit to those who ask him*" (Luke 11:11-13 NIV)! Even though humans are not without flaws, we generally know how to love and treat our children well. However, the Lord God practices love towards us on a much higher level than we can ever achieve.

We can see this same dynamic in forgiveness. My children are a part of the family. I would like for them to always make exactly the right decisions, but in no way do I expect that. Their mistakes and faults do not cause them to quit being a member of my family. In fact, I cannot tell you what it would take for them to cease being a part of the family. I can only guess what my limits of forgiveness might be. I do know that there have been countless examples of extraordinary forgiveness of a child by a parent. A gripping example is that of Kent Whitaker, a dad in Sugar Land, Texas. Several years ago, an attacker in his home wounded Kent and murdered his wife and youngest son. Later Kent discovered that his oldest son had arranged the attack. Despite that inconceivable horror, Kent was later able to forgive his son (Kent Whitaker, *Murder by Family*, 2009). Could I forgive in such a situation? It would be hard to be definitive on that, but I certainly understand the power of love that allows that to happen. Our love and ability as humans to forgive can be great. Comparatively, though, God's can be amazing! We must expect that the awesome Heavenly Father can and does forgive completely. Limiting him in any way by saying he only forgives partway is unacceptable.

Restoration Back to Family

We will extend the family concept by looking at the parable of the Prodigal Son (Luke 15:11-32). The younger son was a part of the family but chose to forego that relationship. Later he returned home. The father at once accepted the prodigal son back into the family despite some protestations. This is a great example of God's complete forgiveness. Forgiveness is all about reestablishing relationships. It is not about the sin act itself. Forgiveness says the wrongdoing will not be punished by banishing the other person from the relationship. Here, the younger son is forgiven and received with open arms as a family member. The father would not even discuss the sins with the son, because they were irrelevant to the reunion. Paul put this well for us when he said: "*When someone becomes a Christian, he becomes a brand-new person inside. He is not the same anymore. A new life has begun!....For God was in Christ, restoring the world to himself, no longer counting men's sins against them but blotting them out*" (2 Corinthians 5:17, 19 TLB). To be restored or to have peace with God, we must allow God to obliterate the offense as if it had never happened. It is not brought up again. It is not recorded in a log. It is not later used against us. It is removed completely from the records. The sin or offense that caused the separation is no longer important.

That may seem a little hard to understand and accept. Think about your own relationships. My friends and my family do not always act the way I want them to act. Occasionally, they might do something very painful to me. In spite of that, our relationship is much more important than anything that might threaten those bonds. They treat me the same way. We do not dwell on those things that have caused pain or bring them up again. We do not sit around and say, "Hey, remember how tacky you were at the game?" or "When you ignored me five months ago that really hurt." Instead, the offenses have been overlooked. They are not a part of the relationship. They have been erased. If we can achieve that level of forgiveness in our personal relationships, think how much more God can do the same for us.

Recently, a friend who had experienced some marital troubles described a counseling class he was taking. One of the big takeaways from the teacher was the concept of an endgame. The teacher encouraged the students to ask themselves, "What is my endgame?" whenever an argument or a tense situation arises in a marriage. "What am I trying to accomplish and what would I like to see happen in the long run?" If the answers are that I love my spouse and I want to have a good marriage, then all the other stuff can be overcome. It is the same with our Lord. The other hindrances can be overlooked if the endgame is right. The endgame is a relationship between God and us.

It is significant that the father in the parable refused to even consider taking back his estranged son as a slave or servant. God's forgiveness always involves a full restoration of the relationship. It must be complete because we are either in his family or we are not. The Lord calls us his children because we are fully children. We are part of the family because we have chosen that and because God has forgiven all our efforts to not be a part of the family. The younger son was family. He was 100% forgiven because that is the very nature of God.

What is Forgiveness?

What had been the young son's sin? He rejected his family and left home. In the same vein, what was the father's forgiveness? It was the overlooking of the sins that caused the son to be estranged. Forgiveness carries the sense of giving up the power or desire to punish in order to achieve the result of reconciliation. The details of sin and the number of sins are unimportant, because all the sins must be forgiven to achieve a total restoration. Let us imagine a person wanting nothing to do with God and therefore rejecting him. The person declares himself or herself an atheist. In addition, our example has a good job, contributes to the community, and is a good citizen. Another person also rejects God and wants nothing to do with him. This person gets into crime and lives a violent life. Both persons want to come back to God. Forgiveness must be complete in either case for reconciliation to happen. To forgive and restore each person, God must forgive every sin. There is no other way. Partial forgiveness would not work. By his very nature, God cannot have half of a relationship with us. He cannot welcome us back but ask us to live in the garage. In the same way, there is no purgatory or half-hell. We are either at home with the Father, or we are away from home. We are part of the family, or we are not.

Legally, it works the same way. Suppose I commit three murders and I am facing the death penalty. I request a pardon from the governor. It would do no good for her to pardon me for two murders and not the remaining one. Why?

I would still be executed for the unpardoned crime. The only way I can be saved from the death penalty is to be totally pardoned of all the offenses.

Punishment serves many purposes in our human systems. The general thought is that punishment can be a deterrent to further crime, a rehabilitation opportunity for the criminal, or a way to satisfy our sense of justice. We therefore want to be careful to fit the punishment to the crime. For the Supreme Judge, it is different. He is not that concerned with the size of sin or the number of sins. Rather, God is concerned with the person and how any sin could sever our relationship with him and with other people. If we are counting individual sins and trying to fit the punishment to a specific sin then, sure, each sin would be evaluated on its own merits (or demerits). Sin is not the issue. We are the issue. When God sees us turn away, he extends his hand to us. Upon our return, he makes us free from the guilt as well as the punishment.

All In

What advantage is it for God to forgive 90% of our sins and still hold a grudge on 10%? What good is it if he erases every sin out of our life's book except for a couple? As humans, we forgive imperfectly. We forgive some people and not others. When we do forgive, it is sometimes only partway. We also tend to have an incomplete understanding of what it means to forgive. For many of us, forgiveness is only about putting a bad situation behind us and moving on. We may even qualify our forgiveness by saying, "I will forgive you, but I can't forget the offense." In contrast, the Lord God always offers complete forgiveness. He must be all in. There is no middle ground with God. When he forgives, he forgives all the way. It is as if the sins had never happened. We typically wish the record of our deeds to be heavily skewed with the good acts outweighing the bad. However, there are no bad deeds in the book. In fact, there is no book at all. God's love means he keeps no record of wrong. Sins or wrongs are never brought up later or held against us in any way.

When we come back to the Father, we are returning to family. We are at home. The Lord does not care what we have done, where we have been, or when we arrived back. He cares that we are at home. I think it so sad that people say they will come to Jesus Christ only when they straighten up their lives. That is based on a faulty understanding of mercy and grace. We are never going to do enough good things to make up for the bad things we have done. It does not matter though. We have a Father who will forgive every sin and forget everything we have done. *"Don't tear your clothing in your grief, but tear your hearts instead. Return to the Lord your God, for he is merciful and compassionate, slow to get angry and filled with unfailing love. He is eager to relent and not punish"* (Joel 2:13 NLT).

Those Sins, too?

What is the worse sin you can think of? Serial Killing? Genocide? Child abuse? Torture? Sex enslavement? We are inclined to separate wrongdoing into different degrees of severity. As a result of such categorization, we, therefore, believe any forgiveness is related proportionately. Worst sins must be harder to forgive than the lesser sins. We do not have a problem with the Lord's ability to forgive our petty shoplifting. Can he forgive our murdering as well? The answer is yes, although it may be difficult to accept. We can study and debate all we want to about big sins and little sins, but arguments are moot. Any sin, big or little, terrifying or unnoticeable, that separates us from God can be forgiven by God. He will forgive if we choose to be with him.

Despite sometimes being taught that all sins are equal, we still tend to view sin by degrees. Certainly, human societies do make a distinction between felonies and misdemeanors, seeing some offenses as more major than others. It must be that way in one sense. Societies need to fit any necessary punishment or consequences with the size of the wrongdoing. That is logical. The problem is that when it comes time for mercy or forgiveness, we continue in the realm of categorizing offenses. It seems natural for us to want to rate offenses and thereby match our corresponding efforts at forgiveness. I might forgive you for forgetting my birthday but not for abducting my child. That is an extreme example, but I think it makes my point. Because we think in terms of gradients, we apply that to how the Lord might view our sins. Surely, he can forgive my white lies or missing a church service, but how in the world can he forgive my prostitution or abusing my family? From our human perspective, we always need to know the offense or crime so we can determine the punishment or perhaps the degree of mercy. Here is the neat thing. God never asks, "Where have you been?" or "What have you done?" Those questions are irrelevant to him. He is asking, "Where are you now?" and "Do you want to be with me?"

In the story of the Prodigal Son, we do not know the number of sins or the kinds of sins. That oversight does not diminish the power of temptations and the resulting sin choices. Sins of any kind and of any number can be potentially dangerous and possibly fatal. The danger of individual sins always comes in the context of separation. In this case, the real problem is the Prodigal Son's leaving home. The particular sins involved in his journey away from home are not the point. In the same way, the focus of forgiveness is the father's total forgiveness resulting in the acceptance of the son. We must be careful that we do not limit the power of the blood of Jesus Christ to only small sins or a small number of sins.

The Things We Omit

When I was growing up, church attendance at worship services was considered vital. We dutifully went every time the church doors were open whether we felt like it or not, whether we were in town or not, and whether the Cowboys were playing or not. Faithful attendance, as we referred to it, continued although the Bible says nothing about Sunday night or Wednesday night. Later in life, I heard a joke that gave me some comfort. The joke goes like this: It was Judgment Day and there was a long line of people waiting at the pearly gate. The queue moved slowly, especially for one group of friends who were far back in line. Occasionally, they would hear from way up near the entrance someone yelling, "Oh, thank you. Thank you. Yahoo!" Finally, one person in the small group volunteered to make the journey to the front to see what was going on. After a while, she came running back, extremely excited. "It's great," she exclaimed, "Wednesday nights don't count!"

This story introduces us to the question of what people would refer to as our shortcomings. Earlier we said that sin is a negative word related to what we do not do. Sin is NOT doing as God would have us do or NOT being as God would have us be. Sin is contrary to our ideal of being created in the image of God. Often, we see sin as doing something wrong, committing a crime, or behaving badly. What about the times we just fail to do what is right? Consider the crime found in some jurisdictions known as failure to stop and render aid. Pretend you are driving lawfully and hit a person who steps in front of your car. You did no wrong because the accident was not your fault. If you continue driving down the road, you could be charged with failure to stop and render aid. The theory says it is the responsibility of citizens to do the right thing of helping the person. That is a specific case, but we are confronted with similar dilemmas in our spiritual lives. We are challenged not only in the cases of doing something wrong but also in the cases of not doing something right. The preachers of my youth liked to make sure we understood that. They would expound that while the sins of commission were terrible, the sins of omission were just as bad. The text for the sermon was almost always "*Whoever knows the right thing to do and fails to do it, for him, it is sin*" (James 4:17 ESV).

While this verse teaches a valid lesson about making good choices, it can also be misapplied. It is easy for us to concentrate so heavily on our oversights that we create a constant picture of failure. We can see ourselves as not having a chance. Some of us might just sneak through life by avoiding the lures of the dark side but feel accused of not doing enough good things. We can take a pie to a sick neighbor today, but what if we miss out doing the same three days from now? And what about the sick people we never get around to? If we are not careful, we can create an endless list of unaccomplished good deeds. We not only condemn ourselves but others as well for what is not done or what is not said. For our purposes, we should stick with the good news God forgives every sin of omission. That is huge.

Missing the Mark and Imperfections

He forgives us for not being good enough. He overlooks all our imperfections. Some of us have heard sin defined as missing the mark. That definition is not found specifically in the Bible but is from the etymology of the word. When sin is merely seen as missing the mark, then no wonder so many of us feel guilty all the time. We can never be as pure as God. We can never make the best choices every time. We can never do good 100% of the time and avoid harm 0%. If the goal is perfection, then we all fail quite often. Occasionally, we get lucky and score a bulls-eye, but most of the time we are just trying to stay on the dartboard. Nowhere in the Bible does it say the Lord expects you or me to never make a mistake or never do harm. Since we do not expect that kind of perfection of our family and friends, why do we think God expects it of us? He created us, so I am quite sure he knows our limits.

If we were without fault, we would not need God at all. The very essence of forgiveness recognizes that we have inadequacies and that we do make intentionally bad choices along with inadvertent mistakes. Our coming back to the Lord is the admission we need him for us to be complete. If we are honest, much of the guilt we constantly feel is not so much about actual sin but about a perception that God prefers error-free lives. We want to feel forgiven but, at the same time, think God still wants us perfect and is often disappointed when we are not. What we fail to understand is love and forgiveness are almost always about a "despite of" as well as a "because of." If we learn anything from the characters of the Bible, it is that God can and does forgive imperfections. As at Mt. Sinai, we can remember, "*Yahweh! The Lord! The God of compassion and mercy! I am slow to anger and filled with unfailing love and faithfulness. I lavish unfailing love to a thousand generations.*" (Exodus 34:6-7 NLT).

Incorrect Beliefs

This is probably a good time to talk about our beliefs. In my fellowship, what you believe has historically been critical. Sometimes correct beliefs seemed to rank right up there with correct actions. Conversely, incorrect beliefs could be incredibly significant. They could even be deadly. Any wrong belief was considered a sin. Not believing the right things or the right doctrine would keep you separated from God, as much as any other sin. Does God forgive our incorrect belief? We would have to say yes, if we accept that God can and does forgive all sins. If he can pardon murder and abuse, he can certainly do the same for our mistaken beliefs. People commit sins with all kinds of intentions. Sometimes they do something openly and defiantly. At other times, they do so unintentionally or subtly. The same happens with our beliefs. While we may be openly stubborn or aggressively inflexible, we may also believe or not believe something due to ignorance or false information we have received. Regardless, *believing imperfectly* falls under the same umbrella as *acting imperfectly*. As we often do not do something we should do, we also fail to believe as we should believe. The beauty is that God forgives all imperfections, whether that be imperfections of actions or of belief. Will people who have committed adultery show up in heaven? Yes. Will people who have kidnapped children be there? Yes. Will people who have erred in what they believe have access to paradise? Yes. Quite frankly, we all need to rejoice in that. Why? It is because my beliefs most certainly differ from yours in some way.

What about false beliefs? Does not the Bible condemn some false teachers? Certainly! Both Jesus and other Christians leaders dealt directly with false teaching. Like sin, false teaching can be problematic for us. The fact that God can forgive both sin and incorrect beliefs does not make either one acceptable. Just like sin, the main problem with incorrect or false teaching is that it can separate us from God. Many of the warnings aimed at different teachings are aimed at those that directly challenge the deity, power, or love of God. That explains why peddlers of wrong teaching are sometimes referred to as "antichrists (1 John 2:18)."

With sin, it is possible at times for a person to influence others towards the same sin. However, with false teaching, other people are almost always affected. Thus, any false teaching that leads to the separation of other people from God or even makes it more difficult for them to accept or follow God will be condemned. Jesus was particularly strong towards those teachers who not only kept themselves from the Kingdom but also prevented others. *"You cross land and sea to make one convert, and then you turn that person into twice the child of hell you yourselves are"* (Matthew 23:13, 15 NLT)! Our concern here is not so much about what makes false teaching bad but what makes it forgivable. Like sin, no matter how harmful, false teachings can be forgiven when the perpetrators repent and turn to God. On the other hand, those who advance theories or dogma that attack the essence of God or who promote ideas that prevent other people from experiencing God, show themselves as not in the Spirit.

Another question comes up when we talk about God being able to forgive wrong beliefs. Can we be forgiven for not even believing in God due to our choice or even to our ignorance of his existence? Although the question might appear to border on the realm of how many angels can dance on the head of a pin, we must take it seriously. We will answer the question by saying it is not about how many sins or what kind of sins God can forgive. Rather, it is about what the Lord will do to have a relationship with you or me. He will do a lot and will forgive everything, but it is always dependent on the aim of our being with him. He can open the gate and invite; we must walk in. Lack of belief in God and his Son negates our acceptance of such invitation. It keeps us from even getting to the question of forgiveness because it constitutes rejection of any forgiveness. Interestingly, that helps us segue into the next question.

The Unforgivable Sin

I have made some bold statements about God forgiving all our sins. Is there a Biblical exception to that assertion? Perhaps. Once, after Jesus healed a man with a demon, he made a statement that both concerns and baffles Christians: *"So I tell you, every sin and blasphemy can be forgiven—except blasphemy against the Holy Spirit, which will never be forgiven. Anyone who speaks against the Son of Man can be forgiven, but anyone who speaks against the Holy Spirit will never be forgiven, either in this world or in the world to come"* (Matthew 12:31-32 NLT). Some might think this unforgivable sin contradicts what I have been saying. First, let me clarify something. I never said that God will forgive all sins. I said that when he forgives us, he forgives all our sins. There are sins that will never be forgiven just as there are sinners that will never be saved. In fact, there may be more unforgiven sins out there than forgiven ones. Forgiveness of our sins is always in conjunction with our entering into or back into a relationship with the Lord. You cannot have any forgiveness unless there is alignment with God on our part. Forgiveness and relationship happen at the same time.

Having said that, let's deal specifically with the question: "Is there one sin that is the exception to the idea that God can and does forgive all sins?" The answer is yes. Jesus says that blasphemy or speaking against the Holy Spirit will not be forgiven now or ever. Admitting that blasphemy is a concept we do not always fully grasp, we can get some comfort by looking at the context. The Pharisees had earlier accused Jesus of doing his work through Satan. This is the key to what is being addressed in the story. In response to these remarkable accusations, Jesus made it clear that his power came from the Spirit and that his works involved bringing people into the kingdom. *"But if I am casting out demons by the Spirit of God, then the Kingdom of God has arrived among you"* (Matthew 12:28 NLT). The blasphemy against the Holy Spirit is the deliberate, open-eyed rejection of known truth. The people had watched with their own eyes as Jesus performed healings and mighty works by the power of the Spirit. Attributing those works to the evil one and thereby rejecting the works of the Spirit would not be forgiven because those things cannot be forgiven. They cannot be forgiven because one cannot side with Satan by promoting the works of the Lord God as the works of the Devil and still be with God. It is back to our either/or choice which Jesus confirmed, *"Anyone who isn't with me opposes me, and anyone who isn't working with me is actually working against me"* (Matthew 12:30 NLT). Equating the works of Jesus Christ to the works of Satan is the same as proclaiming Jesus is Satan and working against the Lord. Jesus said, *"Make a tree good and its fruit will be good, or make a tree bad and its fruit will be bad, for a tree is recognized by its fruit"* (Matthew 12:33 NIV). Make a choice. Recognize the works of Jesus Christ as originating through God's Spirit or reject them.

In Conclusion

I may have had some of you at "forgives all sins." However, I do believe that there are several Christians who still feel God is holding back on them. They think God has removed all sins, but he could go back into the trash bin and pull some sins out. They do not realize that their book of sins will be blank because God forgives all sins. He keeps no record of wrongs.

In the next chapter, we get into an area that might be a little harder for some of you to swallow. I certainly hope none of you have skipped this present chapter about the first tenet. For the second tenet to click it must be backed by your agreement on the first. If you still do not believe the first tenet, then please stop and spend some more time with it and work through it to see why you are having trouble. Otherwise, enjoy and continue.

6 Will Future Sins Be Forgiven?

> Phil Connors: "That was a pretty good day. Why couldn't I get that day over, and over, and over?"
>
> (*Groundhog Day*, Dir: Harold Ramis, Columbia Pictures, 1993)

IN THE FIRST TENET OF FORGIVENESS, we said that when God forgives, he forgives all our sins. Although we discussed the completeness of his forgiveness, we did not mention much about the timing. Timing is important. When does God forgive sins? Does he only forgive past sins, or does he also forgive current and even future sins? Those are great questions that can be answered as we explore the companion piece to the first precept.

One Time Only

This second tenet of forgiveness is that Jesus Christ only died once for our sins. This probably seems rather simple, much like the first tenet. Taken together, these two tenets can have real life-changing effects, even for you now. We want to address the idea that Jesus Christ only died once and only needed to die one time. This also is talked about several times in the Bible. For example:

- "*For Christ also suffered once for sins, the righteous for the unrighteous, to bring you to God. He was put to death in the body but made alive in the Spirit*" (1 Peter 3:18 NIV).
- "*Otherwise Christ would have had to suffer many times since the creation of the world. But he has appeared once for all at the culmination of the ages to do away with sin by the sacrifice of himself*" (Hebrews 9:26 NIV).
- "*For we know that since Christ was raised from the dead, he cannot die again; death no longer has mastery over him. The death he died, he died to sin once for all; but the life he lives, he lives to God*" (Romans 6:9-10 NIV).

I like the way the writer of Hebrews put it, particularly in chapter 10. He said in earlier times priests had to make sacrifices every day. They did so because the important annual sacrifice made by the high priest was not completely effective. If the yearly sacrifices had worked, the priests would have stopped them and "*the worshippers would have been cleansed once for all*" (Hebrews 10:2 NIV). In striking contrast to these annual sacrifices, "*we have been made holy through the sacrifice of the body of Jesus Christ once for all*" (Hebrews 10:10 NIV). Jesus Christ is our forever high priest that made his sacrifice only once. Our priest "*offered for all time one sacrifice for sins*" (Hebrews 10:12 NIV) and through this "*one sacrifice he has made perfect forever those who are being made holy*" (Hebrews 10:14 NIV). The writer went on to say that God will forget our sins and lawless acts and "*where these have been forgiven, there is no longer any sacrifice for sin*" (Hebrews 10:18 NIV). What this means is that Jesus does not have to die every day. He only died once and that was for all time and for all people. The power of that death was for those who lived 2,000 years before Jesus Christ and for those of us who live 2,000 years after him. Most importantly, it means that when the Lord forgives in Christ, he forgives forever.

I used to have a problem with that. The problem was not that Jesus died only once. I certainly did not have reason to believe that he died many times. No, my problem had to do with the timing. I felt I was okay because Jesus' death was a past event, and I was on the right side of history. It happened prior to my life so I was able to profit from that historical event. I used to worry about all those unfortunate people who missed out because they lived before the death, burial, and resurrection of Jesus Christ. What was to happen with those people who were following God earlier than the crucifixion? I thought they had no hope since they had lived their entire lives with no knowledge of Jesus Christ. How could a future event that had not even happened affect them now?

God's Time

What I have since discovered is that God's time is different from our time. In fact, God likely exists outside of time altogether although he does interact with us. We are told that to Yahweh "*a thousand years is like yesterday, like a few hours in the night*" (Psalm 90:4 ERV). The longer we live the faster time seems to move. Similarly, units of time seem to get smaller as we age. For example, Christmas seems like an eternity away for a child, but for an old person, it arrives too quickly. Of course, the differences in perspective might have to do with whether we see Christmas as a wonderful miracle of new gifts or whether we see it as a day we must manage the relatives. More than a mere perspective, it is simple math. A year for a 5-year-old is 20% of his/her life; for grandpa, it is likely less than 2%. A year for an older person just seems smaller.

However, we are not merely dealing with differences in the feeling of time. Rather, the Sovereign Lord is not bound by human time constraints at all. It is not that he has lived a long time although he is the Ancient of Days, after all. Also, it is not that a thousand years is a relatively short period if one has been around billions and billions of years. No, a day to God is as a thousand years because neither a day nor a thousand years are relevant to him. He has not lived a day and he has not lived a thousand years. He just is. Time is something he invented for us. He had no beginning or end. God did not start or stop. With the Lord, there is no human sense of was not, now is, and someday will not be. God works within our understanding of time, but he is not limited by it in any way. We are the ones confined inside a cosmic aquarium, thereby living in a series of events with a beginning and an end. As we understand it, God is not in the aquarium. He is outside of it. He is walking around it, so to speak. The Creator can be above the aquarium of our existence, under it, or even in it. On the other hand, he is not contained by it.

It is the same with time. Imagine your life as a movie. It has a beginning and an end with several events in between. In my day, there was no rewind. The movie started at a certain time and ended at a certain time. If you came late to the movie theater, you simply missed part of the movie. It was gone. There was no going back but only going forward. We could not watch the movie again unless it played later. Times have changed. The marvels of technology allow us, with a click, to be at any part of the movie. We are not bound by a start time or an end time. We can make it live over and over. We can watch at any time of the day and on any date. In our lives, God is the one with the remote. We are in the movie. We have only one shot, but he has an infinite number of shots. He can be before the movie of our life, after the movie, or during the movie.

For the Maker it is irrelevant when something takes place but only that it takes place. Following World War II some soldiers served on a Pacific island to administer the local government. One day an inhabitant of the island ran up to the commander of the unit and was very agitated and excited, saying, "Hurry my cousin has been shot and killed." The commander and a few troops interviewed some villagers and decided a murder had been committed. The perpetrator had never been brought to justice. However, the killing took place many years earlier. For some, this story strikes as a little funny. How can people suddenly be so excited about an ancient event? The answer lies in how time is viewed. Westerners see time as a journey that moves along in a linear fashion. We live in a present that is very real, but we are moving into a future that is about to be very real. Both are important. The past is important but not as important since it is gone. In linear thinking, we move away from the past.

The islander had a different world view. For him there was a very uncertain future, so the future was not very important. The future had not happened and for him, the future will never happen. His present was the present of today only. The past was extremely important for the islander because the entirety of his past life experiences composed who he was. For him, the past grew, and he moved into the past as more of his life was there. In other words, the islander's life was made up of a rather small present, no future, and a large past. He kept no calendar and no timepiece. When something happened was unimportant to him. What happened was the thing that mattered. In our mind, a bad crime often loses its importance with the passing of time and sometimes disappears altogether. We think it odd to be excited about a 30-year-old event. For our islander, it was as real and as present as if the event happened yesterday. Why? It had never been corrected.

It helps me then to understand God if I see time more like the islander did and less like a Westerner. There are no time constraints for the Lord God. Jesus died for us, and he only did it once, for all time. It is not when he died, but the fact he died that is important. The one-time event covered the past, the present, and the future. *"This sacrifice shows that God was being fair when he held back and did not punish those who sinned in times past, for he was looking ahead and including them in what he would do in this present time"* (Romans 3:25-26 NLT). The person who lived 2,000 years before the death and resurrection experiences the same effects as those of us who live 2.000 years afterward. *"For Christ died to set them free from the penalty of the sins they had committed under that first covenant"* (Hebrews 9:15 NLT). It does not matter if Jesus Christ died in 33 AD, 5,000 BC, or even if he has not died yet, assuming it will happen at some point. It is that the event happens.

Our Life

Interestingly, that concept does not apply just to humans throughout history, but it applies in the same personal way to your life and my life. God can save me from my sins today, but he can save my whole life through the one death of Jesus Christ. When the Father forgives and saves, he does not just do that for one day or one decade of our lives. Instead, he saves our whole life and forgives us of all sins. We said earlier that God does not selectively forgive a few of our sins. Similarly, he does not selectively forgive sins committed in only one part of our lives. God forgives sins through the one-time death of Jesus and has forgiven us of our sins. What does that mean? The only thing it can mean! <u>He forgave our sins from a year ago, he forgives our sins from today, and he will forgive them a year from now</u>. It might even be safe to say the Lord has already forgiven all our present and future sins. How can we say that? How can we say God will forgive me of future sins as well as past sins? Simply, Jesus only had to die one time. The Hebrew writer said that the Lord God can save completely not only by forgiving all sins but also by forgiving throughout all our lives. *"He is able, once and forever, to save those who come to God through him. He lives forever to intercede with God on their behalf"* (Hebrews 7:25 NLT). He does not have to die a year from now to take care of our sins coming up. He does not have to die again. He died once, and that one-time death covers our entire lives. Whatever power went out from the death and resurrection covered all of history, your entire life, and my entire life. Saying Jesus needs to keep dying to be effective denies the power of his death.

Jesus is the once-for-all-time sacrifice. God does not save piecemeal, nor does he forgive piecemeal. He saves forever. At baptism, all our sins are washed away, and we start with a new slate. Too many Christians think we then begin at once to fill the slate back up with sin. NO! The pages are empty. They are empty at baptism, are empty now, and will be empty tomorrow. We are just as free of sins today as the moment we came up out of the waters. We will be just as free tomorrow and next year. We have seen people laughing and crying at baptism because of the joy of salvation. We can have that feeling every day.

In and Out?

When I was very young, my mom taught me to say a prayer each night before I went to bed. It went like this:

> Now I lay me down to sleep,
> I pray the Lord my soul to keep,
> If I should die before I wake,
> I pray the Lord, my soul, to take.
> (Joseph Addison, *The New England Primer*)

I was okay with the laying down to sleep and with the Lord keeping my soul. I had real problems with dying before I wake. There were many nights the concern canceled out any possible peaceful sleep. At some point, I decided never to pray that again or to teach that to my children. The anxiety of that prayer underscored a common Christian belief. Many of us live in a cycle of sin and forgiveness. We may get up in the morning saved, but then we sin. We ask for forgiveness, accept a dose of salvation, and wait for the next inevitable sin.

There is no scenario like that in the Bible. We are not in Christ one moment and then out of Christ the next. There is nowhere in the Bible that implies that we jump in and out of salvation. Our Father does not say to us, "You are my child today but not tomorrow. You sinned and now you aren't my child." We do not disown our own children daily nor does God his. We are not in the family and then out of the family and then back in again. We are in Christ, and we stay in Christ because the blood of the son of God continues to purify of us of all sin (1 John 1:7). This is what the continuous process of forgiveness is all about.

Some Christians tend to think that forgiveness for sin does not come until we think about the sin, repent of it, and ask forgiveness. When I was younger, I wanted to make sure that I was all prayed up. However, requiring a specific *mea culpa* after every sin or even a blanket confession at night does not make sense for several reasons. No one denies that coming clean through apologies is a good idea. Confession is a reaffirmation of our choice towards God and away from not God. It makes us feel less guilty, but it also helps reestablish a relationship with an offended person. However, confessions are not a magic formula that must be recited to ward off evil. Any stated confession of sin only makes sense in the context of our life goal to be with God. Confession says out loud what is continually in our heart: we want to be with God and do not want anything to get in the way of that relationship. To extend forgiveness to us, God does not require a specific confession every time we sin. Remember the point is that God is forgiving us and not forgiving just a sin. Forgiveness comes willingly from the Lord and takes place through the blood of the One Who Dies Once. Because it is so complete and is for our entire life, forgiveness doesn't stop and start. It is not withheld from us, pending a corresponding request or a good deed. It is important to realize forgiveness does not stop, but it does not delay either. Requiring an immediate confession or a specific act of atonement from us for every sin would mean that forgiveness is either stopped outright or delayed until that confession. In either case, that would mean that we would be in an unforgiven state for periods of our life. The blood of Jesus continually washes us, so we are not in the position of being unforgiven between the commission of a sin and the verbal acknowledgment of such.

Confidence

How can we be so sure that God will forgive me the sin I commit tomorrow? I will go back to the movies. When someone points the gun and says, "You are dead!" technically that is a lie since the victim is still alive at the time of the statement. The bad guy is not saying the victim is dead literally, but that the event is so inevitable that it is as if the death event has happened already. It is the inevitability of the event that is important. Timing is almost irrelevant. It is the same with the timeless Creator who has no beginning or end. He is not eternal in the sense of lasting forever. Instead, he is timeless. That is why we are affected by the event of Jesus' death and not the timing of that death. Whatever happened in the death and resurrection was for all time with no beginning date and no ending date. Jesus Christ did not have to die on day one to be effective for people who have lived or will live on this earth. In the same manner, he did not need to keep dying over and over like a booster shot. It was one death for all time. Whatever confidence I have that God will forgive my sins tomorrow and for the rest of my life comes from knowing Jesus has already died for them and does not need to die repeatedly. Forgiveness of my sins today AND tomorrow is a done deal. There is no worrying about or hoping the Lord forgives. He does.

God is faithful. He will not let us down. When my wife and I were married, we promised mutual faithfulness. It is technically possible that either of us could be unfaithful. One can never say never when it comes to humans. Yet, you know what? My wife's possible unfaithfulness is not a concern to me at all. I do not spend one-minute worrying or thinking about it. The likelihood of her unfaithfulness is so small it qualifies as an impossibility. Speculative events do not affect one thing I do or think. For example, I could get hit by lightning walking out my door tomorrow, but that is in the realm of near impossibility. With God, we are not even dealing with infinitesimally small odds associated with the chance of nature or the whelms of humans. God said that Jesus Christ only had to die once for me and if I am in Christ his blood will continue to wash away all sins. A promise by the Almighty will never be broken.

A Journey?

We sometimes make the mistake of thinking that we are moving on a journey towards the Lord. If we think in terms of linear time, our earthly stay might be seen as a journey. Often, I hear Christians talk of how we will be with God someday or how we are growing closer to God. Contrary to that view, I believe we are not on a journey towards God in the sense that we are here and expecting someday to be there with him. If we choose to think of life in sojourn terms, it is helpful to envision the Lord is in a car with us on a trip. We are not going in the direction of the Eternal One. Instead, we are traveling with him on the journey of earthly life. We do not need to talk about going to heaven or being saved someday. We are saved now. We are with the Savior now. Christians are as saved now as they ever will be. We will not be saved at some point in the future since we are already saved.

Even the idea of talking about getting better or being better can get us caught up in a similar problem. Granted, there is nothing wrong with wanting to grow as Christians in love, goodness, knowledge, and self-control. However, we must be somewhat careful in talking about improvement if we think the Lord requires it to keep our relationship. God does not demand you to be better than you are right now. If you are kinder or more loving tomorrow, that is great. He loves you and accepts you today just as you are. Growth and improvement may be part of our being in God's image, but they are not requirements for salvation. Compare that to our interaction with friends and family. At any one moment, we accept them the way they are. If they improve in the future, we will still accept them. If not, do we expect to drop the relationship? I believe we can understand the human element, but it is hard at times to extend the same assumptions to the Lord. Sometimes we cannot grasp that we are okay the way we are because we cannot appreciate the extent of unconditional love. Continuous forgiveness makes us complete at this very moment. It does not demand more from the past or from the future.

Christians can get hung up on the idea of satisfying God. We know he is without fault, and we know we want to please him. However, we have a time problem. We are always comparing our present self with our future self. We know who we are and what we do today. In the back of our minds, however, there is the lingering thought that we could be better and do better tomorrow. That is usually true. Because that possibility exists, we easily conclude God expects improvement from us to be satisfied. Since he might expect a better us, logically that means he will not have full satisfaction until we become better and act better in the future. That thinking is absurd. The future does not exist. The past is gone and irretrievable. What we have is the present and it is the present that counts with God. We can certainly say with confidence that the Lord is completely satisfied and pleased with us today if we are presently in a relationship with him. Forgiveness has taken care of any sins up to this moment and no sins have been committed yet in the future. The Father does not have a house made up of some family members he likes and some he does not. If he is dissatisfied with a person, it is because that person has left the family and chosen the sinful, not God path. Of course, anyone has the choice to return and receive the forgiveness of God. If, on the other hand, we have chosen God, he is satisfied with us. *"Come near to God and he will come near to you"* (James 4:8 NIV).

The Number of Sins

We were taught breaking just one law was always enough to condemn us, and any sin might cast us into the nether world. Those ideas led to the simple conclusion that we are all separated from the Almighty because everyone has committed at least one sin. Some people even posit the one sin that causes you or me to be a sinner was not committed by us. Instead, they say the sin that caused our personal downfall is the one sin committed by Adam and Eve! The Bible does not explicitly say that the first sin committed by us always condemns us. That concept of the power of one sin seems to have been developed from two thoughts. One, there are Biblical examples of punishment meted by God for one act of sin. I am not sure it is fair, but it is easy to extrapolate the punishment in those cases to our eternal punishment. Two, scholars contrasted the Almighty's purity and goodness with our seemingly despicable nature. Given that, preachers agreed that one sinful act would be unacceptable to a holy God. They explained one slip is all it takes in any case. It was assumed we were all sinners because everyone committed at least one sin. While these two thoughts might have some merit, it still is difficult to accept that a single sin always condemns us. As mentioned, there is nothing in the Bible that directly teaches that. I am sure that theological debate will continue.

Even if we might not theologically reject the "one-sin-always-equals-condemnation" equation, many of us often do so practically. No matter what the scholars might teach, most Christians believe that committing multiple sins is always worse than committing one sin. In other words, we usually believe the numbers count. Accordingly, we feel that while God might be able to forgive one or two sins, many sins make the task more difficult. Some of us even feel there is a breaking point for God in which we use up the forgiveness allotment. We suspect committing too many sins will cause him to give up on us. These fears need to be examined.

Jesus touched on the number of sins when the woman washed his feet with perfume. He told this story to his dinner host: *"A man loaned money to two people—500 pieces of silver to one and 50 pieces to the other. But neither of them could repay him, so he kindly forgave them both, canceling their debts. Who do you suppose loved him more after that"* (Luke 7:41-42 NLT)? The answer was obvious to any human listener. The debtor with the bigger debt would likely be the most responsive. Jesus drove the point home by saying of the woman, *"She was forgiven many, many sins, and so she is very, very grateful"* (Luke 7:46 MSG). Gratitude and not judging others are lessons to be learned from the story. We also learn something related to how God views numbers. The problem is the debt itself and not the number of coins making up the debt. The Lord does not keep a tally to determine whether he will forgive or not. There is no limit to the number of sins God forgives. The amount might concern us, but it does not affect God.

Addictions

When we talk of continual forgiveness, invariably the objection arises over those sins that are repeatedly indulged in via some form of addiction. In other words, we might accept forgiveness where a person commits a sin today, a different sin tomorrow, and another type of sin later. It is harder to get our minds wrapped around the scenario in which a person commits one sin over and over. In human terms, we see a difference between a one-time offender and a repeat offender.

We even make great allowances for that in our court systems. The hurt done on the fifth time seems less forgivable than the hurt done the first time. We take seriously the old saying "Fool me once, shame on thee. Fool me twice shame on me." Is that true for God also?

Consider this encounter: "*Then Peter came to him and asked, 'Lord, how often should I forgive someone who sins against me? Seven times?' 'No, not seven times,' Jesus replied, 'but seventy times seven'*" (Matthew 18:21-22 NLT)! Peter's frustration with repeat offenders is certainly something we all have had to confront. Quite frankly, Peter was likely feeling comfortable because he was ceding that forgiving seven times surely would cover the obligation. After all, seven times was very generous and the perfect number to boot. Other than for a few members of our family, how many of us have forgiven another person for the same offense seven times? When you think about it, that is a lot. Almost unbelievably, Jesus says we must forgive 490 times! There is no limit to forgiveness, and he is talking about one human forgiving another. How much more would God's forgiveness for us be?

Given our two tenets of forgiveness, that makes perfect sense. God's forgiveness covers sins for all time and covers sins regardless of size or severity. There is no reason to think God cannot or does not overlook the sin we commit for the 49th time or the 490th time. After all, the problem is not when a sin is committed. The problem is the effect of any sin in potentially separating us from God, whether we did that sin only once or a thousand times. The Father can forgive any number of sins, even repeated ones, if such forgiveness leads to reconciliation. I hope you caught the "if". "If ifs and buts were candy and nuts, we'd all have a Merry Christmas" (Don Meredith).

I have been trying to convince you that God forgives all our sins all the time. With the *if*, I am starting to hedge my bet. There is a reason for that. God will not and cannot forgive all sin. God does not forgive us simply to spare us the fires of hell. He forgives us for the purpose of reconciling the world to himself. Despite what some people believe, we have a choice in whether we want to participate with God or not. As per our softball analogy, we need to sign up and play. If we do not want to be with God and live the life he created for us, then forgiveness has no point. In other words, if we choose not to be with God, God allows that choice. He allows us to remain in sin, separated from him.

The answer to the question of repeated or addictive sin hinges on this idea of choice. What are the intentions of the person? That is important in our social life and is especially important in our legal processes. Was the crime premeditated? What was the purpose of the crime? The Almighty must make the same types of distinctions because the goal reaches beyond the sin itself. In Numbers, there is an interesting passage that gives us some insight: "*If one person sins unintentionally, he shall offer a female goat a year old for a sin offering. And the priest shall make atonement before the Lord for the person who makes a mistake, when he sins unintentionally, to make atonement for him, and he shall be forgiven. But the person who does anything with a high hand, whether he is native or a sojourner, reviles the Lord, and that person shall be cut off from among his people. Because he has despised the word of the Lord and has broken his commandment, that person shall be utterly cut off; his iniquity shall be on him*" (Numbers 15:27-28, 30-31 ESV). The hypothetical here deals with two different cases involving an unknown sin. In the first case, the sin is unintentional and can be forgiven. In the second case, the sin, although the same as the first, cannot be forgiven because it is a sin done with a "*high hand*" ("*defiantly*" NIV; "*brazenly*" NLT). Think of Stands with a Fist, the heroine in *Dancing with Wolves*.

The forgivability in the two cases is not about a different type of sin since the sin referenced is the same in both cases. Rather, the forgivability has to do with intention. In other words, God is saying there is a giant difference in forgiveness based on the choice of the person committing the sin. Paul indicated the same division of motives when he said of his own situation, "*Even though I was once a blasphemer and a persecutor and a violent man, I was shown mercy because I acted in ignorance and unbelief*" (1 Timothy 1:13). This confirms the idea that intent is intertwined with sins consequences and does affect forgiveness. The writer of Hebrews weighed in, "*If we deliberately continue sinning after we have received knowledge of the truth, there is no longer any sacrifice that will cover these sins*" (Hebrews 10:26 NLT). To deliberately continue sinning is to make the choice to be different from and to walk away from the Lord. We could debate the varying degrees of intention because motives cannot be limited to either mistake or defiance. For our point, it makes a difference whether we want to continue our relationship with God or whether we are in rebellion against him.

That is true with all the sins we commit as Christians and applies equally to repeat sins or sins of addiction. When we covenant with the Maker to live the life we were created for, we accept a complete lifestyle change. Paul assured us, "*But that's no life for you. You learned Christ! My assumption is that you have paid careful attention to him, been well instructed in the truth precisely as we have it in Jesus. Since, then, we do not have the excuse of ignorance, everything—and I do mean everything—connected with that old way of life has to go. It's rotten through and through. Get rid of it! And then take on an entirely new way of life— a God-fashioned life, a life renewed from the inside and working itself into your conduct as God accurately reproduces his character in you*" (Ephesians 4:22-24 MSG). We are promised that the Spirit will work in us to move from the old life of sin to the new life of the Spirit. As dramatic as the conversion event may seem for some, the practical transformation from the old life can be a process for others. When we recognize that processes take time, we learn to be careful in judging too quickly the intentions of the individual who battles with addictions. It is easy for us to categorize someone's repeat offenses as a sign of insincerity.

On the other hand, it is similarly easy for people to deny their own sins and addictions or to minimize the impact. In fact, it has been popular in the last few decades for the world to characterize addictions as diseases for which the individual has no control. Be aware the Bible never says that. The Bible does recognize there are outside forces that affect us, but the ultimate responsibility for our choices, sin or God, rests with us. We are assured that God will not put temptations on us greater than we can resist. That is why it is so important for Christians to turn constantly to God and to other Christians for support. A person's sin can affect the group.

While it is true that each day for us can be a great day, there was one day in history that was truly beautiful. That was the day Jesus was resurrected. It was the most beautiful day not only because it was the day sin was conquered, but also because we can relive that day every day. The one-time sacrifice of Jesus Christ makes sure that complete forgiveness is truly total because it covers our entire life.

7 What is Our Cost Again?

> Charlie Anderson: "Lord, we cleared this land; we plowed it, sowed it, and harvested it. We cooked the harvest. It wouldn't be here—we wouldn't be eating it—if we hadn't done it all ourselves. We worked dog-bone hard for every crumb and morsel. But we thank you just the same anyway, Lord, for this food we're about to eat. Amen."
>
> (*Shenandoah*, Dir: Andrew McLaglen, Universal Pictures, 1965)

IF PEOPLE KNOW THE DANGERS OF SIN and understand that forgiveness offers them a path out, it follows that most people would rush to get in line. That is not the case. Forgiveness that covers all our sins for all our life is often met with a surprising amount of resistance. There are myriad reasons why a person might completely reject God and his offer of forgiveness. Those reasons would best be addressed in a separate discussion. However, I would like to respond to those who do choose God yet have a hard time taking full advantage of the divine benefit. We will look at some of the concerns most expressed by Christians who are reluctant to move from partial forgiveness to complete forgiveness.

Cheap Grace

Growing up, I was imbued with what I consider to be a fair sense of right and wrong. Not only was that sense strong, but it was also unambivalent. Doubt and fence-riding were neither encouraged nor expected. Rewards were there for being right, although praise for that was not always expressed. Being wrong resulted in punishment. Amends could be made, and mistakes overcome, but such outcomes almost always came at a cost. Thus, I felt forgiveness let people off the hook and mercy made me feel like a cheater. It would not surprise you that grace was not a word used much at home or in my church during my early years. Churches change, though, just as societies and cultures change. Granted that usually comes with a dose of pain and resistance. Words like grace, mercy, and forgiveness became more common in my church during my high school and college years. Such new language was generally welcomed among the Christians I called brothers and sisters. On the other hand, as new ideas come and gain acceptance they often do so with certain qualifications. Thus, it was with the increased acceptance of grace in my church. We had always believed in grace and forgiveness, even if the words had not been easy on our tongues. As grace terminology floated more and more throughout the classrooms and auditoriums of my youth, we made sure that it carried a qualifying banner: "No Cheap Grace!" Church members uncomfortable with a new emphasis on grace could be more accepting, provided everyone understood that it came with a cost. Grace might be okay, but cheap grace was not tolerated.

7 What is Our Cost Again?

In trying to qualify grace as cheap or costly we run into a dilemma. The fact is both phrases, cheap grace and costly grace, are oxymorons. Grace, by its very definition, is a gift. To say God extends grace is simply to say that the forgiveness and the resulting salvation are something we neither pay for nor deserve. Forgiveness is a gift from God. A gift is something that is given to you by another. It is not paid for or else it would not be a gift. We do not exchange money, time, or work for a gift. If we did swap anything then the gift would become trade goods or compensation and would no longer be a gift. Because of that, a gift is always free for the recipient. It can be neither cheap nor expensive. On the other hand, a gift might be either expensive or cheap for the giver depending on how he or she acquired it. Perhaps it was free for the giver and is merely a regifting! No matter what the gift might have cost the giver, the gift is always free to the receiver. In the same way, grace can never be cheap for us or costly for us. We did not deserve it, nor did we do anything to pay for it. It is not cheap. It is not expensive. It is free. *"You should look for the Lord before it is too late. You should call to him now, while he is near. Evil people should stop living evil lives. They should stop thinking bad thoughts. They should come to the Lord again, and he will comfort them. They should come to our God because he will freely forgive them"* (Isaiah 55:6-7 ERV).

While grace never involves a cost for the receiver, for God it is a different matter. He paid, as it were, the ultimate cost. *"When we were utterly helpless, Christ came at just the right time and died for us sinners. Now, most people would not be willing to die for an upright person, though someone might perhaps be willing to die for a person who is especially good. But God showed his great love for us by sending Christ to die for us while we were still sinners*" (Romans 5:6-8 NLT). In my favorite verse of all time, we are told Jesus Christ died for us while we were not acting properly. His forgiveness was extended in the middle of our rebellion and while we were alienated from him. "We see, then, that [grace] is *costly* because it cost God the life of his Son: 'ye were bought at a price,' and what has cost God much cannot be cheap for us. Above all, it is *grace* because God did not reckon his Son too dear a price to pay for our life, but delivered him up for us" (Dietrich Bonhoeffer, *The Cost of Discipleship*, 1937). That reminds me of the simple, but powerful song:

> He paid a debt He did not owe. I owed a debt I could not pay.
> I needed someone to wash my sins away
> And now I sing a brand-new song: Amazing Grace.
> Christ Jesus paid a debt that I could never pay.
>
> My debt He paid upon the cross. He cleansed my soul from all its dross
> I tho't that no one could all my sins erase
> But now I sing a brand-new song: Amazing Grace.
> Christ Jesus paid a debt that I could never pay
> (Ellis J. Crum).

The Obligation of Receiving Gifts

We recognize that God is perfectly holy, and we compare our sinful condition to him. We do seem like worms who are not worthy of forgiveness, as the song once suggested. We might accept forgiveness but have a hard time with unconditional forgiveness.

7 What is Our Cost Again?

It is often difficult for us to accept any gift unless we can reciprocate. Receiving a gift creates an obligation and puts us in a debtor position. It makes us unequal with the giver and that is often discomforting. A good example of this is gift-giving in some parts of Asia. There, the art of bestowing and receiving gifts encompasses a whole set of traditions and social responsibilities. It is very important who you give gifts to and how much is given. Problems might develop in both personal and business relationships if too much is given or too little. The color of the package makes a difference. It even makes a difference whether the gift is a check or cash. If cash, it should be crisp and unfolded and not wrinkled and old. It further matters whether you are giving an odd amount or an even amount. One central key is this: If you are given a gift, you should also repay the gift with something of equal value. Paying back either too little or too much can cause significant embarrassments and relationship strains. For example, you would never want to give a boss a bigger gift than she/he gave to you.

While the West tends to be less strict than Eastern traditions, gift-giving anywhere can be problematic. Most of us can remember Aunt Clara showing up to Christmas with an unexpected gift for us. We then grease the skids of an apology by mumbling, "I did not get anything for you yet." That may be why my brother once suggested that we simply exchange $20 bills at Christmas! It is awfully hard for us to accept gifts. That is strange since from birth we are regaled with the honor and joy of receiving gifts. And yet, receiving gifts is awkward for several reasons. The main reason is that we want to be equal to others as much as possible and we do not want to be obliged to another person.

When it comes to God, we cannot help but compare ourselves to him. We even wear bracelets that say WWJD or What Would Jesus Do? That should be an encouragement to better choices and a higher standard, but often it is a reminder of the distance between God and us. We know ourselves and that knowledge often holds dark thoughts and actions. We feel those things can never be undone or rectified. To accept a gift of a million dollars when we only have a dollar to return seemingly puts us in a hole we can never get out of. Happily, the beauty is that gifts are never to be repaid. They are, by definition, gifts. With other people, we hem and haw around with something like, "I can't let you pay for dinner." With the Lord, we might say, "I am not good enough yet, but when I am, I will be back." All those responses are feeble attempts to pay back the obligation and try to create equality with the giver. With God, there is no obligation. There is no tit for tat. Thankfulness is the best response and often the only response. What we sometimes call mere gratitude is the essence of our worship to a Maker who needs no payback. Paul encouraged us to be "*giving thanks to the Father...in whom we have redemption, the forgiveness of sins*" (Colossians 1:12, 14 ESV).

Free Rides

You can probably see how this discussion on grace and gifts points us to why it is so hard for many to accept God's forgiveness. The problem is that non-Christians, as well as a disturbing number of Christians, still function under the belief that forgiveness comes to us because of how good we might be. The view that we must pay for forgiveness taints every facet of our lives and affects how we view ourselves and others. Amazingly, the same fundamental problem can produce two different outcomes. One of these negative results is that some people accept that they themselves are forgiven, but other people are not. This is what Jesus so often condemned among religious people. They could accept forgiveness for themselves because of their diligence in following the law. The religious folk easily condemned others when they did not follow the law in the same way or to the same degree. Jesus asked rhetorically, *"Why do you notice the small piece of dust that is in your friend's eye, but you don't notice the big piece of wood that is in your own"* (Matthew 7:3 ERV)? Too often we hold others to a much higher standard than we do for ourselves.

It is sometimes hard for us to grant leniency if we view any forgiveness as a free ride. This is seen starkly in the attitude of Jonah. When asked by God to extend the hand of mercy to the enemies of Israel, Jonah reluctantly complied. However, he was not happy. *"I knew that you would forgive the people of this evil city, so I decided to run away to Tarshish. I knew that you are a kind God. I knew that you show mercy and don't want to punish people. I knew that you are kind, and if these people stopped sinning, you would change your plans to destroy them. So now, Lord, just kill me. It is better for me to die than to live"* (Jonah 4:2-3 ERV). Jonah could not understand mercy that did not also bring justice to those who sin. To him, it seemed arbitrary and unfair that others received a get-out-of-jail-free card just because they were lucky. We might feel the same if we think we deserve mercy, and the other person does not. Recall the older brother in the story of the prodigal son who considered himself the faithful one. Another example includes the workers in the vineyard who worked all day for their day's wage while others got paid the same for only an hour's work (Matthew 20:1-16). How often do we Christians relate only to the offended party in these parables rather than to the seemingly favored ones? In those cases, God's answer is always the same: mercy and forgiveness are who I am. What may seem unfair or arbitrary to humans (because we can often be egotistical) is consistent with the nature of God. *"Are we saying, then, that God was unfair? Of course not! For God said to Moses, 'I will show mercy to anyone I choose, and I will show compassion to anyone I choose.' So it is God who decides to show mercy. We can neither choose it nor work for it"* (Romans 9:14-16 NLT).

This tendency to view ourselves as forgiven, without extending the same to others, is not just demonstrated in individuals. Groups also exhibit the same characteristic. It is easy to think that if our group is made up of select people with special privileges then it follows that our standing in the group must correspond with believing and/or acting as our group does. We then want to protect the policies, traditions, and practices of the group and avoid anything that might conflict with them. The whole premise of this book is that forgiveness is bigger and more comprehensive than we may be able to understand. That can be heady but also a bit scary. It can make one doubt not only previously held beliefs but also might cause a Christian to appear to be accepting something different, perhaps even false doctrine. You might want to embrace some of the new ideas I have conveyed, but fear or skepticism might cause you to back off. Let me give an example of how this might work. As mentioned earlier,

Christians are exclusive in their view of salvation. Most Christians would then run from any idea of universal salvation, a belief that all people everywhere will be saved. However, the simple statement that Jesus Christ died for all people for all time can sound a whole lot like universal salvation. We might then be skeptical of any new ideas concerning forgiveness because we do not want to be seen as embracing something like universal salvation, which our group might not accept.

Another example involves groups within Christianity. As individuals we do not share the exact same beliefs with other individuals. In the same way, groups do not share the same beliefs with other groups even if those groups exist within a broader assembly (such as Christianity). If I am a Christian and you are a Christian and we do not believe 100% the same, then it follows that two Christians over here probably don't agree 100% with the two Christians over there. I was raised with a negative view of the doctrine of "once saved, always saved." If you are like me, you can see how the idea of forgiveness that applies to our sins in the future as well as to the sins of the past might be resisted. My point is not to debate the specific beliefs like universal salvation or once saved, always saved doctrine. Rather, my point is to show that many of us can miss out on the God-given, Biblical wonders of forgiveness while trying to protect or deny certain doctrines. Be careful of that.

Back in the 70s, there was a popular book entitled *I'm Okay; You're Okay*. It had its distractors, but it generally promoted acceptance and tolerance. Interestingly, Christians often regard tolerance as a dirty word. We interpret the word to mean giving up principles and lowering standards. We sometimes are so passionate for truth, right, and law that it is hard for us to make room for different beliefs or different ways of living. When we see that God does not require perfection, it becomes easier for us to accept others without trying then to match our ideals in everything.

We do have a problem. When outsiders are questioned about their feelings towards Christians and the church, one consistent answer is that people feel judged and unwelcomed. That is also commonly named as one of the top reasons people leave the church. That is as amazing as it is alarming. No one should be able to understand and accept others more than Christians. That should be one of our hallmarks rather than one of our negatives. Jesus constantly condemned religious people who could not show tolerance to anyone who was not exactly like them. There may be several reasons why religious people are often not accepting of others, but certainly, one to consider is that although we profess and believe in God's forgiveness, we really have a difficult time internalizing that. In other words, we often do not forgive because we do not believe God has fully forgiven us.

Consider this parable: *"The Kingdom of Heaven can be compared to a king who decided to bring his accounts up to date with servants who had borrowed money from him. In the process, one of his debtors was brought in who owed him millions of dollars. He couldn't pay, so his master ordered that he be sold—along with his wife, his children, and everything he owned—to pay the debt. But the man fell down before his master and begged him, 'Please, be patient with me, and I will pay it all.' Then his master was filled with pity for him, and he released him and forgave his debt. But when the man left the king, he went to a fellow servant who owed him a few thousand dollars. He grabbed him by the throat and demanded instant payment. His fellow servant fell down before him and begged for a little more time. 'Be patient with me, and I will pay it,' he pleaded. But his creditor wouldn't wait. He had the man arrested and put in prison until the debt could be paid in full. Then the king called in the man he had forgiven and said, 'You evil servant! I forgave you that tremendous debt because you pleaded with me. Shouldn't you have mercy on your fellow servant, just as I had mercy on you'"* (Matthew 18:23-30, 32-33 NLT)? This parable does not need a lot of explanation as it clearly shows a bold rebuke to our unforgiveness of others.

What about Forgiving Ourselves?

The first result that comes from thinking we must pay for forgiveness is that we forgive ourselves but not others. A second result, seemingly the opposite in effect from the first result, is that some of us accept that others are forgiven, but we ourselves are not. We can have a difficult time accepting God's mercy because there are terrible sins available to us and those sins can cause dire consequences to us, our families, the church, and the whole world. When we are the ones who do the harm through sin, it becomes personal, and we can feel a huge amount of shame and guilt. In some cases, we can try to rectify the damage, but that is often impossible to accomplish. After all, "the moving finger writes and having writ, moves on. Nor all your piety nor wit shall cancel half a line" (Omar Khayyám). When we find we cannot erase the event from ever happening, we are left holding the bag. We stew in our guilt, trying to continually find a way to administer some equalizing pain to ourselves, the proverbial eye for an eye. This may be true even though God has forgiven the sin and is requiring no punishment. But we cannot let it go. That is why we speak about forgiveness of ourselves and how hard that is for some people.

In one sense, "forgiveness of ourselves" is an odd phrase. If the primary goal of forgiveness is reconciliation, then how can we reconcile ourselves to ourselves? The answer comes in understanding forgiveness of our self is not about reconciliation. It is largely about giving up the self-punishment we inflict. We know we have hurt others and we know we cannot make that completely right, by either making the sin not happen or by an equal pain to ourselves. Interestingly, this problem with not forgiving ourselves often is in the context of someone not forgiving themselves despite having been forgiven by the offended party. Therefore, we might say, "I know so-and-so has forgiven me, but I can't forgive myself" or "I believe God has forgiven me, but I can't forgive myself." My contention, however, is that when we say we cannot forgive ourselves then the underlying problem is that we really believe God has not forgiven us. We can intellectually believe the Lord forgives, especially that he can and does forgive even very bad things in others. However, we often feel that our own sin, coupled with our intentions and perhaps our continuation in sin, is so severe that a good and perfect God just cannot forgive and overlook the stain.

We cling to the belief that we still are not good enough to be with God. But we are! God's forgiveness makes us good enough. Remember that we are made perfect or complete by the one sacrifice (Hebrews 10:14). Whatever barrier to a relationship with God which comes through sin and any potential resulting punishment are both abolished in the death of Jesus Christ. The forgiveness from above cancels out any need to forgive ourselves.

Cannot Trust Ourselves

Christians balk at any expanded forgiveness because we distrust our motives. We fear that if we accept full forgiveness of all sins that might cause us to give up on church and doing good. Some of us fear deep within our actions are driven by guilt or fear of hell rather than by love and altruism. Paul addressed this directly because early Christians had the same concern we do. They saw forgiveness and mercy as the opening of the floodgates. It is commonly thought that if people are not held accountable and punishment can be avoided, they may choose to not do good. Paul said some Christians, seeing how amazing grace was, might suggest we should just keep on sinning to keep the gifts and rewards coming. His response to such ideas was quick and strong: *"Of course not! Since we have died to sin, how can we continue to live in it? Or have you forgotten that when we were joined with Christ Jesus in baptism, we joined him in his death? For we died and were buried with Christ by baptism. And just as Christ was raised from the dead by the glorious power of the Father, now we also may live new lives"* (Romans 6:2-4 NLT).

Like those earlier Christians, we too ask, "If God forgives everything, why should we try to do good or to improve?" For a Christian to even dare ask such questions suggests we do not get it. We must understand the motives that come from being with God. We do not do good or treat others with love because of fear of hell. We do so because we have been molded by God for those purposes. How can a person who has experienced life changes and is now walking in the light of God's steadfast love think about doing harm or sinning? We do not act out of fear of punishment because we are motivated by love. *"And as we live with Christ, our love grows more perfect and complete; so we will not be ashamed and embarrassed at the day of judgment, but can face him with confidence and joy because he loves us and we love him too. We need have no fear of someone who loves us perfectly; his perfect love for us eliminates all dread of what he might do to us. If we are afraid, it is for fear of what he might do to us and shows that we are not fully convinced that he really loves us"* (1 John 4:17-18 TLB).

A friend passed along this explanation. When we were babies, we were not capable of obeying or disobeying our parents. We were completely dependent upon their care. We grew to a point, however, when we became capable of choosing to obey or disobey. At that point, we knew there would be punishment for disobedience and the fear of that punishment caused us to obey. As we matured, we began to understand that our disobedience truly disappointed our parents. Our primary motive to obey changed over time from fear of punishment to wanting to please our parents. Finally, as we matured, we came to understand that what our parents wanted of us was true, just, and right. That became the primary motive for our obedience.

Admittedly, some fear and some guilt can drive Christians to occasionally act as they should. Those things may never go away completely. Certainly, fear and guilt could be encouragements to repentance, particularly in the cases when a person has yet to experience forgiveness. On the other hand, as we grow in our Christian life, we are changed in such a way that love becomes the greater force behind our actions. We are better off to rely on our love for the Lord and for others as primary motivation rather than any negative motivation. The Father trusts us to do exactly that because he willingly eliminates fear and guilt from our lives through forgiveness and acceptance. Remember that *"there is no fear in love, but perfect love casts out fear"* (1 John 4:18 ESV).

Humility or Arrogance?

Christians are caught between the proverbial rock and hard place. On one hand, we try to hold ourselves and other Christians to a higher standard than we might if there were no God. We preach the high road in all facets of life. On the other hand, we do not care to be labeled as holier-than-thou because of those expressed standards. People can sometimes accept that other people might have more talent, more wealth, more beauty, and even more goodness. However, no one likes to be shown up by any superior attributes or even by any implied superior attitudes. Christians might be able to champion moral goals without pushback if they do so carefully. However, anything that intimates in any way that the other person is lacking in those desired moral qualities will be quickly rebuffed. The problem is always one of perception. For example, is a wealthy person always ostentatious every time he or she chooses to wear expensive clothing or drive a fancy car? Or do the rest of us only consider it wealth-flaunting when the rich talk excessively or reveal their wealth in places we consider inappropriate? It is a fine line.

The same problem exists when we discuss goodness and morality. How can Christians wear their morality in such a way it does not seem to cast judgment on others? One common solution tried by Christians is to make sure others do not perceive any moral superiority in us by constantly declaring our moral equality. "We are not perfect, of course." "We are like anyone else." "We are just sinners." To me, such statements arise from either a misunderstanding of what it means to be good or evil or, more likely, from false humility. If the latter, then we really walk on dangerous grounds. What might innocently be seen as an aid to better relationships with non-Christians ends up being counter to one of our core values, the trust in a God who has forgiven us through Jesus Christ. In other words, <u>claiming to still be a sinner basically denies the power of forgiveness to change our lives.</u> One cannot walk in the light as he is in light if we still see ourselves as creatures of darkness. Of course, a Christian is not morally superior to a non-Christian. In the same way, a Christian is not better on some good-evil axis. Nonetheless, there is a difference between Christians and non-Christians. The difference is that we have chosen to follow God through Jesus Christ and non-Christians have not. The choice is only possible because of the forgiveness granted us. Forgiveness is a powerful part of our lives and allows for countless benefits. We cannot toss that away by fearing someone who rejects those benefits might think us arrogant.

7 What is Our Cost Again?

As a concluding note, let me caution against using the ubiquitous "I am just a sinner" as an excuse. When convenient for them, the world does like to throw our standards of morality back in our faces. They are particularly delighted when a deacon or priest is discovered in some sexual or abusive situation. That seemingly confirms what many believe: the church is full of hypocrites. Our standard response is to proclaim that we are not perfect, thereby insinuating that the world should not hold us to higher standards. While we are not perfect, we only hurt ourselves by trying to lower expectations. God created us in his image. When we do err or sin, his overwhelming love grants us unconditional forgiveness and keeps us in his presence. We should embrace what that means. We hold ourselves to high standards because they are divine standards. We may not always act and love perfectly, but we certainly have no problem with reaching for that. When we are not as loving, caring, or accepting as we would like, we should not simply admit imperfection. Rather, we should say, "You are right. We do believe and preach love. When we fail to be perfect that is our humanness, but our godliness simply calls us to keep reaching for the highest order and his forgiveness allows it to happen."

While the world rejects forgiveness as part of the whole God package, an alarming number of Christians seem to partake in a weakened form. We need to stop kicking against the goads. We need to stop resisting the concept of full forgiveness. We need to leave behind the insecurities, doubts, and feelings of guilt. Instead, we must embrace the power of the Spirit to embolden us. *"The Spirit and the Bride say, 'Come.' And let the one who hears say, 'Come.' And let the one who is thirsty come; let the one who desires take the water of life without price*" (Revelation 22:17 ESV).

8 What is In It for Me?

> Eric Liddell: "I believe that God made me for a purpose...for China. But he also made me fast. And when I run, I feel his pleasure."
>
> (*Chariots of Fire*, Dir: Hugh Hudson, Warner Bros. and 20th Century Fox, 1981)

I HOPE I HAVE GIVEN YOU enough new perspective so that you can see how your life can be changed. Each reader will have his or her own answers to the question: What does God's forgiveness mean for me? I can only try to convey to you some of the sense of wonder that has changed my life.

Frees Us from Real AND Perceived Guilt

There are different definitions of guilt. When I say *real guilt* I am using the definition: "the fact or state of having committed an offense, crime, violation, or wrong, especially against moral or penal law" (Dictionary.com, n.d.). Real guilt says you did something wrong whether you admit it or not, whether you feel remorse about it or not, whether you are caught in the act or not, or whether a jury decides you are guilty or not. We all have done bad things that no one else knows about. We are guilty of that crime or offense, nonetheless. Sometimes people commit a wrong or crime, but the jury or judge says they are not guilty. They are guilty in a real sense but not a legal sense. Real guilt and legal guilt are not necessarily the same. As we know, the flip side is that sometimes a person can be pronounced guilty and sent to prison but did not commit the crime.

I say that because when God forgives, he forgives the real guilt. It is not just a foregoing of punishment. Rather it is as if the crime or sin had never been committed. That is why God says, "I will not remember your sins." There is no record. We are not acquitted or pardoned of sin, that is, released from prison. Rather, we are judged as not guilty by the biggest judge of all. We are absolved of guilt. The record of the deed is expunged and no longer exists. It is not marked through or covered up. It is erased and double deleted. There is no longer a record because there is no longer guilt. God keeps no record or list of your sins to compare them against a good deeds list. When you stand before God in the final day and the books are open your book of bad deeds will be blank. Your sins have been blotted out and eliminated.

However, you could still be counted as guilty by fellow humans and could be punished in some form for your actions. Being blamed by others does not mean that God also blames you. There are certainly washed and forgiven Christians sitting on death row for crimes they committed. Societies cannot pardon every criminal who professes repentance and acceptance of the blood of Jesus Christ.

We can feel guilty even when we are not. It happens all the time. That is why actually many people confess to crimes they did not commit. Sometimes, when pressured with created evidence, people start to feel guilty. I believe Christians often just feel guilty. They might ask forgiveness for sins committed unknowingly or beat themselves up over good deeds they have not accomplished. Perhaps they constantly compare themselves to exemplary Christians they know or to a Jesus Christ who never seemed to make even a tiny mistake or allow a random, dirty thought. Preachers constantly push us to do better, which always implies our guilt and shortcomings. It is hard to feel guilt-free if we cannot accept that God loves us without condition and accepts us today and tomorrow. We sing "Just as I Am" followed by a sermon on how we need to improve. No wonder so many ex-members talk about the guilt they found at church. Do not get me wrong. Growth and maturing are parts of our Christian life just as love, kindness, gentleness, and self-control are. Reaching some mark on the growth chart as a requirement for God's favor is not a part. My problem is when we think God will not accept us fully into the fold unless we are better than we are right now. Now contrast that to the Christian who understands complete forgiveness comes because God genuinely loves us. Imagine not even having the question of God's love arise. It does not have to be imagination because we can all live guilt-free.

Frees Us to Walk into the Presence of God

Any forgiveness involves, to some degree or other, three results: giving up the bitterness, foregoing punishment, and restoring the relationship. In the best scenarios, all three outcomes will be present. Suppose your friend lies behind your back and you stop talking to them. After a while, the friend calls you up and apologizes so you decide to smooth things over. You stop your pouting, and you then go on with your mutual texting or fishing together. In this case, you are no longer bitter or mad, you have stopped the punishment of non-communication you had imposed, and your relationship is likely as good as ever. Of course, situations needing forgiveness can vary considerably and so does the degree of forgiveness as expressed in the three possible outcomes. Sometimes the results of forgiveness are not complete. Suppose a stranger robs you. At some point, you get tired of "swallowing the poison" and you determine to give up the grudge of hate. You drop the charges, figuring a long-drawn-out and expensive trial is not worth it. You move on and forget about it, for the most part. Seemingly, you have given up the punishment although you might not be sad if the thief did happen to get a little jail time. Likely, you have not created or restored any relationship with the thief and probably have no desire to. Have you forgiven? Perhaps so. Perhaps not. At best, it is partial forgiveness. As humans, we often believe forgiveness can take place even without relationship building. In fact, most books on forgiveness seem to emphasize the giving up of the bitterness and the punishment, treating any restoration of a relationship as mere gravy. I do recognize that full restoration between humans is not always possible and not always desirable. Having said that, we do tend to use any such restoration exceptions as excuses for the times we just do not care to work that hard to restore relationships.

  With God, forgiveness does not work the same. For one, he does not have the same emotions we have nor is he controlled by them. Thus, it is hard to imagine him as pouting or full of bitterness and needing to "get over it." Secondly, his emphasis is always on the restoration of relationship with the foregoing of punishment being a subset to that. Given that most of this book has discussed sin and punishment and even that the two core chapters on forgiveness have dealt mostly with God's passing on punishment for our sins, you might think it strange to now be saying our avoiding hell was never the point. That is precisely what I am saying. Avoiding giving punishment is not the goal for God and avoiding receiving punishment is not ours. Rather, the beautiful thing about God's forgiveness is that it allows us to enter a secure and everlasting relationship with him. God's forgiveness allows us to walk into the presence of God and to call him Our Father. We are told God *"has brought you into his own presence, and you are holy and blameless as you stand before him without a single fault"* (Colossians 1:22 NLT).

    Early followers of God would not dare enter the Holy of Holies since it represented the presence of Yahweh. Only the high priest could go in one time a year and only then after extensive sacrifice. On the day of crucifixion, the curtain to the Holy of Holies was ripped open from top to bottom. The writer of Hebrews, in contrasting the people's position with Yahweh at Sinai and our current position, put it well, *"You have not come to a physical mountain, to a place of flaming fire, darkness, gloom, and whirlwind, as the Israelites did at Mount Sinai. No, you have come to Mount Zion, to the city of the living God, the heavenly Jerusalem, and to countless thousands of angels in a joyful gathering. You have come to God himself, who is the judge over all things. You have come to Jesus, the one who mediates the new covenant between*

God and people, and to the sprinkled blood, which speaks of forgiveness instead of crying out for vengeance like the blood of Abel" (Hebrews 12:18, 22-24 NLT).

That event signifies that we have access to God in ways never imagined. When we limit God's power to forgive it is like we do not want to go through the door. All this talk of entering the presence of God metaphorically describes that we have a relationship with God. It is only through forgiveness that we can know God and he can know us. Paul agreed, *"All the things I once thought were so important are gone from my life. Compared to the high privilege of knowing Christ Jesus as my Master, firsthand, everything I once thought I had going for me is insignificant—dog dung. I've dumped it all in the trash so that I could embrace Christ and be embraced by him. I didn't want some petty, inferior brand of righteousness that comes from keeping a list of rules when I could get the robust kind that comes from trusting Christ—God's righteousness. I gave up all that inferior stuff so I could know Christ personally"* (Philippians 3:8-10 MSG).

Understanding that God completely forgives us takes us back to the core of our confidence. So often, we are timid because we do not have full trust in the salvation of the blood of Jesus. We think we do not have anything to offer the world except to try to compete with it in some way. We tout our programs, our worship, and our belonging while avoiding the one thing that sets us apart from every other group—full salvation from sins. Forgiveness and the resulting access to God is the answer for the world, but we want to keep it hidden. What would happen if we could finally say with Paul, *"For I decided that while I was with you I would forget everything except Jesus Christ, the one who was crucified*" (1 Corinthians 2:2 NLT)?

Frees Us to Truly Experience Love

When I read of God's forgiveness, the first inclination is to apply that to me personally. There is nothing wrong with that. However, forgiveness has meaning beyond just you and me and can extend potentially to everyone else. God does forgive us of all our sins throughout our lives, but he also can do the same for other people. Once we realize that God forgives other followers of all their mistakes, sins, and imperfections that frees us up to do the same. We then can feel the full force of God's love because we can share with others that same love.

We know what forgiveness can do for our mental health. In fact, most books on forgiveness emphasize how forgiving others sets us free from hate and bitterness. And there is no denying that power. However, it is not just about you or me and how we feel. Forgiveness of others, Christians and non-Christians alike, allows us to experience love to its infinite degree because, as we know, love is about giving and not receiving. When we are young, Christmas was all about getting and the excitement of receiving. As we grow older, we realize that it is when we experience giving that we finally understand the spirit of love.

The Bible is clear that we are made in God's image. What does that mean? Certainly, it does not mean that we look like him. Rather it means that we own, or potentially own, the divine qualities that make him God. We are not God nor are we gods, although we have within us the ability to love as God does, to be kind like God is, and to forgive as he forgives. When we act toward others as God acts toward us, we are mirroring him and being what God created us to be. Paul stated it well: "*You must be made new in your hearts and in your thinking. Be that new person who was made to be like God, truly good and pleasing to him*" (Ephesians 4:23-24 ERV).

That is why our actions and reactions to other people are so tied up with our interaction with God. In the model prayer, Jesus said, "*Forgive us our debts, as we also have forgiven our debtors*" (Matthew 6:12 NIV). I never felt comfortable with this because I never wanted God to be forgiving me like I forgive others. I want him to forgive me better than I forgive others. This whole deal about tying God's forgiveness of us with our forgiveness of others is so important that Jesus felt a need to clarify. He added a footnote to the model prayer and said, "*If you forgive other people when they sin against you, your heavenly Father will also forgive you. But if you do not forgive others their sins, your Father will not forgive your sins*" (Matthew 6:14-15 NIV). The explanation seems to confirm my fears: if I do not forgive others than God does not forgive me. What is that saying about unconditional forgiveness? Is God limited in what he can do by our actions? Not really. This is not talking about what God can or cannot do. Instead, it shows our treatment of others is closely tied to who we are in Christ Jesus. God forgives us but does so in the same spirit we forgive others. In our forgiving others, we experience as closely as possible what it means to be in the image of God. We experience love to its fullness when we are giving and not just receiving. If we are not practicing love, kindness, and forgiveness, that shows we are not being as God intended.

I like Jesus' explanation in the Message: "*In prayer there is a connection between what God does and what you do. You can't get forgiveness from God, for instance, without also forgiving others. If you refuse to do your part, you cut yourself off from God's part*" (Matthew 6:14-15 MSG). Interestingly, this may also connect us with the forgiveness of others and not just our own forgiveness. "*If you forgive anyone's sins, their sins are forgiven; if you do not forgive them, they are not forgiven*" (John 20:23 NIV).

God's complete forgiveness must change you dramatically in the way you treat others. Christians, including you and I, should be the most forgiving, accepting, and tolerant people in the world. Why? It is because no one has experienced divine forgiveness to the same degree that we have. No one knows the joy we know. No one understands the full power of unconditional love as we do.

Are you separated from anyone in your life right now because they did something to you? Can you name one person you will not talk to or who you avoid? Do you hold a grudge and think badly of a single person? I do not know what your personal situation is, but you must ask a couple of questions. One, is God willing to forgive this person? If God can forgive a person, I would be very wary of withholding my forgiveness. Two, how does this person's wrong to me compare to the wrongs and sins God has forgiven me? It may be the offenses are not as big as we think. Imagine Jesus hanging on the cross and making a list of people you do not need to forgive.

Imagine standing over a person who has wronged you. Then imagine the Lord handing you a stone.

Frees us from Insecurity and Doubt

A few months ago, I heard a dear sister say, "I hope I make it to heaven." She has been a follower of the Lord for over 75 years and is still wondering if she is going to make it. I told her, "You're in. You're in the family of God. You don't have to worry about that anymore." There is no lingering doubt when we realize and accept that God forgives all our sins all the time. We are freed from the insecurity because recognizing forgiveness means accepting that God fully cares for us and does not wish us harm. It is a glorious day when we realize *"God did not send his Son into the world to condemn the world, but to save the world through him"* (John 3:17 NIV).

I want to drive this point home. An amazing number of Christians live their lives in a state of perpetual doubt. Many Christians always look to some future salvation that has not quite arrived. We speak of the possibilities of salvation or being with God rather than the present certainties. "I hope God will save me." "Maybe we will be in heaven." "I want to get closer to God." All these quotes point to some insecurity but can also be signs of a fundamental lack of trust in God. Listen, we are not going to be more saved in the future than we are now. We are not going to be closer to God later because we are not one inch from him now. We are at home with the Father. What can be better than that?

The choice of sin can be a dangerous and frightening thing. It is, after all, what can keep us from the Savior. In direct contrast to the power of sin is the power of God's unconditional forgiveness. Making the point that such forgiveness frees us from sin, takes us out of sin, and changes us from being a sinner to being a child of God does not in any sense deny the dangers of temptations. Instead, such effects of forgiveness affirm the strength of God's love for us. His forgiveness is total and constant. Sin has no control over his forgiveness and therefore no control over us. That is what we trust. It is indeed time for Christians to move away from the language of defeat and into the language of victory. It is time to leave behind the perceived clutches of our past sinful nature and embrace our present spiritual nature. It is time we stop agonizing about future judgment and realize that "*now is the time of God's favor, now is the day of salvation*" (2 Corinthians 6:2 NIV). It is time we abandon the idea God is not satisfied with us. In place of that negative thought, we should be able to feel his pleasure in us. It is time we stand up to those who say we are all miserable sinners locked in daily sin and instead praise God for freedom. It is time to stop dwelling on our sins and start concentrating on God's total forgiveness.

God's love is bigger than anything we can imagine. His forgiveness is complete, erasing sins, wrongs, errors, imperfections, mistakes, inadequacies, bad choices, poor decisions, faults, doubts, and all guilt. All that disappears forever in Christ Jesus. We have moved from death to life, slavery to freedom, and sin to the Spirit. "*May you have the power to understand, as all God's people should, how wide, how long, how high, and how deep his love is. May you experience the love of Christ, though it is too great to understand fully. Then you will be made complete with all the fullness of life and power that comes from God*"

(Ephesians 3:18-20 NLT). Yes, there are things we cannot fully understand. One thing we do know is that we can trust the Lord and the protection he provides to us.

We have made our choice and we can be confident in that choice because the Father has brought us the robe and opened the door. When the door closes behind us, we can know that all our sins have been completely erased. We are now free to fully experience what it means to be in the presence of the Almighty. *"If the Son sets you free, you will be free indeed"* (John 8:36 NIV).

Amen!

Epilogue: Yes...But

> Frankie Heck: "No, I will not be fine in two weeks. I will never be fine. Our son is actually moving to another city for his whole life."
>
> Mike Heck: "So he'll come visit us."
>
> Frankie: "No, he won't. It's very clear we like him more than he likes us."
>
> (*The Middle*, Warner Brothers, Split Decision, 2018)

SOME PEOPLE DISAGREE WITH ME. Occasionally, I encounter someone who merely wants to be argumentative or wants to prove themselves right. For the most part, however, I have found people who ask questions or have concerns about the subjects I cover to be sincere seekers. Most Christians want to believe in complete forgiveness, but from human experience or from what we were taught, we are sometimes hesitant to make a full endorsement. I call these times our "Yes...but" moments.

We hear a sermon on the mercy of our Savior and walk away thinking we believe that. However, in recalling some verse on wrath or hell, we might think the concept of forgiveness needs to be qualified. We read one day about divine forgiveness, but the next day feel frustrated or guilty we said something we should not have or failed to volunteer for the latest event at church. Perhaps, we believe in grace and accept that salvation cannot be earned, but when the subject is brought up in class, we make sure to flip over to James and his take on faith without works. We are always adding our "yes...buts" to the conversation. In other words, we want to put conditions back into the unconditional love of God. We cannot help but think the Father's love is conditioned on our having a love equal to or greater than his. That will never happen. We are better off the moment we realize he loves us a lot more than we will ever love him. John made that precise point, "*True love is God's love for us, not our love for God. He sent his Son as the way to take away our sins*" (1 John 4:10 ERV).

In this epilogue, we address several common concerns others have raised. Often, these objections are accompanied with a scripture to cast doubt on what we said. Some of the questions require detailed or technical answers. Do not let that be distracting and do not get caught up in trying to prove another person wrong and you right. Rather, consider what the Bible teaches. Keep your eyes focused on what makes sense in looking at the overall picture of God's forgiveness, mercy, love, and grace.

I. Frustrations

I didn't stop sinning when I became a Christian. When I think of Christ's blood, I think of that continual process of saving me from my sin. Martin Luther said, "The process has not yet finished." Sometimes that is really frustrating for me. There is a gap between my longing and my living. I see our model Christ and I see myself and there is a discrepancy. Isn't my frustration a normal part of the Christian life?

I appreciate your honesty for two reasons. One, I believe those feelings of frustration are common among Christians. Two, I lived most of my life with the same feelings. I do not anymore. I can now say I am not similarly discouraged and believe there is no reason for any Christian to experience those feelings.

Frustration, by definition, implies that we are trying to accomplish something that is either impossible to do, or is not being done successfully by us. Your continued frustration results from the perceived gap between your expectations for yourself and your actual performance. The pattern of thought goes like this: Christ is our perfect example. It is our goal to be like Christ. We sin and are not perfect. We cannot be perfect. We can never be completely Christ-like on this earth. Therefore, we feel frustrated or even guilty a great deal of the time.

Given that the scenario above makes some sense and is widely taught, why do I say there should be no frustration? The answer is because there is no gap between Christ and us. I heard a teacher recently explain our anxiety by saying we are here, and Christ is there. He presented the accepted view that we are in a process of moving toward our goal. That explanation may seem to logically answer the why of our frustrations, but it does little to give us satisfaction. In essence, the teacher was saying, although we are saved, we are still separated from a perfect Jesus by our imperfections. Thankfully, that is not true. There is no here and there.

There is only here. When we are saved, we are brought into Jesus Christ and into relationship with God. We were saved completely then and are saved completely now. Any existing chasm was bridged by the blood when we were washed and saved. There is no longer a gap between deity and us. Jesus Christ has already crossed it (a little play on words).

You talked about the continual process of salvation. That might sound reasonable. However, we can and probably should say that salvation happens once and is effective all our lives. It does not come as a process moving towards a completion. Forgiveness is not doled out a bit at a time. Whenever we mention the word "process," we are assuming the product has not been finished or that the full results have not been realized. That does not apply to the Christian life. Christians are saved and live in the state of salvation. We have no need to be saved again in the future, since we are presently saved. Paul put it like this: "*If, while we were God's enemies, we were reconciled to him through the death of his Son, how much more, having been reconciled, shall we be saved through his life*" (Romans 5:10 NIV)! In other words, if it is great we are saved even when we were God's enemies, imagine what it will feel like now that we are his friend.

A big problem for us comes because we are taught that our salvation event is merely a beginning. That is why Luther and many others have said the process is not finished in us. However, it is finished in us. There are no requirements left in the future for us to complete our salvation and to bring us closer to God.

Ask yourself: "Am I saved today? Is there something incomplete in me?"

II. New Covenant

According to my Bible, aren't there many scriptures that clearly state the old covenant is obsolete and nailed to the cross? Doesn't that mean we now live under a new set of laws?

Jeremiah 31 and 32 do talk about a new covenant Yahweh will make with the people of Israel. Headings in both chapters (which were placed there by humans) refer to a restoration. This is clear when the Lord says I will bring my people back from being scattered and they will be my people just as I will be their God. The prophecy states that the earlier covenant established when Israel came out of Egypt was broken by the people. The key part relates, *"This is the covenant that I will make with the house of Israel after those days, declares the Lord: I will put my law within them, and I will write it on their hearts. And I will be their God, and they shall be my people. And no longer shall each one teach his neighbor and each his brother, saying, 'Know the Lord,' for they shall all know me, from the least of them to the greatest, declares the Lord. For I will forgive their iniquity, and I will remember their sin no more"* (Jeremiah 31:33-34 ESV).

God says three interesting things concerning the new everlasting covenant. One, the covenant is made with God's house. The writer of Hebrews later quoted this passage and made the point that Moses was a servant in the house, but Jesus was the Son (Hebrews 3:5-6). It was the same house, though. The house of Israel was to be restored. We are told Jesus "*will reign over Israel forever; his Kingdom will never end*" (Luke 1:33 NLT). Neither Jeremiah nor the Hebrews author referred to a new religion or a new people. Two, the new covenant is about forgiveness, which we know is the only way of achieving restoration with Yahweh. "*For I will forgive their iniquity, and I will remember their sin no more.*" (Jeremiah 33:34 ESV). Forgiveness has to do with freedom from sin and not freedom from the law of the Lord. Sin was blocking the relationship between God and his chosen ones. Three, the new covenant is now to be written on the hearts of God's people. Presumably, this contrasts with the earlier covenant delivered in writing on stones. It is notable that there is nothing about the new covenant being a new written set of rules to replace the earlier. Rather, the new covenant is one where forgiveness and restoration replace rebellion and sin. In the new covenant, God's law becomes real in the lives of his people, instead of being ignored by them. Metaphorically it will be "written on their hearts", rather than written on parchment or a stone. The difference under the new covenant is that now "*I will be their God, they shall be my people...and they shall know me*" (Jeremiah 33:34 ESV).

In quoting Jeremiah, the Hebrews writer showed that Jesus is superior to the earlier law. In chapter 8, he (perhaps she) said we have a better covenant because we have a High Priest who mediates better promises. Therefore, the new covenant will improve or replace the old covenant because it will now contain a "better promise" clause. In chapter 9, the writer continued the discussion and gave examples of some of the rules and regulations under the old covenant. It is key that nowhere did the author speak of the old covenant with its written set of laws being replaced by a set of written laws under a new covenant. Rather, the writer explained that the new covenant is better because the sacrifice of Jesus Christ allows for forgiveness for all people. "*Once for all time, he has* appeared at the end of the age to remove sin by his own death as a sacrifice. And just as each person is destined to die once and after that comes judgment, so also Christ was offered once for all time as a sacrifice to take away the sins of many people. He will come again, not to deal with our sins, but to bring salvation to all who are eagerly waiting for him" (Hebrews 9:26-28 NLT). The new covenant is executed with better promises built around the forgiveness found in the one-time sacrifice of Jesus Christ. It is not built around a replacement set of rules.

To your point, we were told, "*You, who were dead in your trespasses and the uncircumcision of your flesh, God made alive together with him, having forgiven us all our trespasses, by canceling the record of debt that stood against us with its legal demands. This he set aside, nailing it to the cross*" (Colossians 2:13-14 ESV). Because of the mention of circumcision and because of other places where Paul discussed the law, some might see this passage as a reference to the abolition of the law. However, given Paul said the law was holy, righteous, and good and Jesus said the law will not pass away, it makes more sense to see something else in play here. More likely, Paul meant we had been under an outstanding obligation he characterized as a legal "handwriting of requirements" or "record of debt." Our choice of sin puts us in a debtor position from which we cannot extricate ourselves. What then allows a cancellation of our debt to take place? Just like in the new covenant allusion, it is all about forgiveness in Christ Jesus. Forgiveness that comes from the death and resurrection is what makes the nailing possible and wipes out any legal obligations as a result of sin. Sin and not the law is our problem and is what needs forgiveness.

We are set free, as Paul explained elsewhere, from the law of sin and death. That must mean any law of sin and death. We are set free not by following a new set of laws but by being in the Spirit. There is no set of laws, old or new, that can set us free from sin. Only the sacrifice of the Lamb can do that. The Holy One did not create a better set of laws. Instead, he offered us a better promise and a better sacrifice.

Ask yourself: "Do I think following the right set of laws will save me? Where does it say we live under a new set of rules or laws that replaced the old?"

III. Christians and Sinners

James writes a scathing rebuke to the "saints" in his letter calling them in James 4:4-8 adulterous people, sinners, and double-minded. Doesn't something sinful remain within us, even though we are covered by the blood of Christ and our sins atoned for?

You are correct that James did refer to some of his readers as sinners. We might extrapolate that all Christians are sinners if we assume James was talking to only Christians. Was he doing that? Who, in fact, was he addressing in chapter 4? Notice the people he called sinners were also named as killers, covetous people, unfaithful people, enemies of God, and people who had not humbled themselves before God. To me, that is strong evidence that James' message was intended to both Christians and non-Christians. While we might feel comfortable, from habit, to call all Christians sinners, I do not think we are ready to call all Christians enemies of God as well. By definition, Christians are not the enemies of the

Lord. People now in Christ are not also all killers and unfaithful. In the same way, we can say that Christians are not sinners either. If James' designations are the basis of an interpretation that all Christians are sinners, we must also conclude Christians are all still enemies of God. Consistency says we cannot just pull out the word "sinner" in making our argument and not include the other names such as "adulterous people." When James pointed out the killers, the enemies of God, and sinners, he was addressing non-Christian readers. From this passage in James, we cannot say "sinners" is a more a universal description for Christians than are the descriptions "killers" or 'unfaithful."

You brought up the ubiquitous theory that sin remains in Christians. One of our problems is that preachers and translators have continued to advance the idea that sin stays with us, not merely as a possible choice on our part but as some force living within us that we cannot escape until we leave this world. It is true sin was once a part of our lives through personal choice and we can even say via descriptive language sin controlled us or was in us. That time of our lives before Jesus has been characterized figuratively as a time of being in the flesh or in the world. We must understand that a literal flesh or a literal world does not control us or cause us to sin. We are the ones who make the choice and are therefore responsible for such choices. Now, however, due to forgiveness we are in the Spirit, and we are not now controlled by the flesh or the world. Interpreters of all sorts just cannot give it up, though. They still want to transform a theology of freedom and confidence into one of continued anxiety and despair.

Stay with me, as I give one small example of how this view is passed on. Paul said to Christians, "*So put to death the sinful, earthly things lurking within you*" (Colossians 3:5 NLT). On face, this verse would agree with your suggestion that sin remains in us. Unfortunately, for you and me, the NLT translators have taken a commonly held interpretation and imposed it on the text. This type of teaching then causes many to be discouraged, even to the point of abandoning their first love. Paul did not say sin lurks within us, as many Christians have been led to believe. In fact, neither the word "sin" or "sinful" is even in the verse! Instead, the original text says, "*Put to death your members on this earth.*" The Greek word for members is one used commonly for limbs, like our arms and legs. Therefore, Paul did not assert a sinful nature lurks within Christians. Rather, he told us to make sure we keep our feet or hands disconnected from our old life of sin. We need to get rid of any possible traps or outside influences. This is reminiscent of Jesus telling us to pluck out our offending eyes to avoid sin. A better translation, and one that gets us nearer the truth and does not suggest we live with an internal, controlling sin nature, is this: "*That means killing off everything connected with that way of death*" (Colossians 3:5 MSG). The NLT translators, like many preachers and theologians, often bring a bias that we still have sin living within us, despite the power of God which removes sin.

I have argued that God's forgiveness washes away or eliminates all our sins. The Lord does not overlook any lingering cancer cells, nor does he leave any behind. We find no comfort in believing that something sinful remains in us. If that is true, then the blood of Jesus has not worked. I do not see how we can have a relationship with the Creator if he chooses not to forgive all sins. After all, it is sin that separates us. Are Christians sinners? I have hopefully made the point that we are not. We were sinners, but we heeded the call of Jesus to repent and have now become righteous. John assured us, "*Whoever lives in love lives in God, and God in them*" (1 John 4:16 NIV). Someday, somebody will need to explain the dubious theology that claims both sin and God live in us simultaneously.

Ask yourself: "Why would the Lord atone for my sins through the blood of Jesus Christ and cover all my sins but still leave something sinful in me?"

IV. Perfection

Doesn't Christ demand perfection! Isn't that our goal, because God is the mark?

If God is the mark, all of us are going to be very disappointed. That is because we are not the Almighty and can never be him. We were created to be in the image of God, and we were made to have relationship with him. Therefore, our goals are those two things and both those things can be accomplished. The Lord does not set for us impossible goals. Granted, being in the image of God and having a relationship with God are goals not achievable on our own. Nevertheless, they are reachable through Jesus Christ. Neither becoming God nor living perfectly without faults is ever within our reach.

If perfection is defined as never breaking the law, never committing a sin, or never making a mistake then I would say that the Creator does not demand perfection. I do not believe God ever expected perfection from us. If we were perfect, we would be God! We do not expect perfection from ourselves or from others. Jesus Christ does not demand perfection from us in any sense of sinlessness or being without faults. He does say we can be complete because his coming allows to be complete. That is possible because his forgiveness overlooks and erases sin.

It is common for Christians to say, "Of course, we know we can never be perfect," while at the same time beating themselves up because they cannot be perfect like God or Jesus. When we claim God is the mark or we need to be like Jesus, we must be careful that those are not just other ways of saying we think we must be perfect. Trying to be perfect then involves our doing more to reach that goal on our own. However, we can never be God or Jesus and are not demanded or asked to do so. One of the main problems is that we often define sin as imperfection. We have been taught that the Almighty created us to be perfect and all of us mucked that up by committing at least one sin. Then we were told God can forgive sins, but he still wants us to attempt to be perfect. It is a vicious guilt-producing cycle.

Suppose we cannot agree on whether the Lord demands perfection or not. Here is the deal. The argument is moot because of forgiveness! I gave up trying to be perfect. That does not make me less perfect than others because we are not perfect anyway. It does generally make me feel less guilty and less ashamed. One Christian thinks he or she must be perfect, and another Christian does not believe that. Which person is better off? I say the latter. In both cases, neither person is perfect, but in the first case the Christian is racked with guilt feelings. Do we believe it is better to be that person who thinks the Lord God demands perfection?

Ask yourself: "Is God disappointed in me if I am not perfect?"

V. Defining Sin

You claim, "Sin is not defined by just breaking the law. Sin's real danger occurs when it leads to separation." Doesn't the Bible clearly define sin: "Whoever commits sin also commits lawlessness, and sin is lawlessness" (1 John 3:4 NKJV)? Doesn't ALL sins, except those repented of, lead to separation?

John did say doing sin is equal to being without law or lawlessness. However, here and elsewhere in the Bible, lawlessness is not referencing something done by Christians but, rather, the state of those who oppose God. In simple, terms, Christians are not lawless because they operate within the laws of the Supreme Being. John described the life outside Jesus Christ in which people are lawless and apart from God. Whoever is doing sin (i.e., engaged in a sinful lifestyle) also tries to function without God's laws. Just as John's description of lawlessness cannot apply to Christians, neither can the corresponding description of doing sin be applied either.

That is why Paul asked rhetorically, "*What fellowship has righteousness with lawlessness? And what communion has light with darkness*" (2 Corinthians 6:14 NKJV)? Lawlessness is the opposite of being righteous and darkness is the opposite of light just as Jesus emphasized that being a sinner and being righteous are opposites. When John then equates doing sin with lawlessness, he is using both expressions to describe the state of separation from God. To be lawless means one is living outside the laws of Yahweh. It is not referring to a single act of disobedience by a person who follows the Savior and tries to live under his laws.

For us, that means we cannot use 1 John 3:4 as a definition for our actions as Christians and we cannot use it to say sin is merely the breaking of a law. If we interpret verse 4 as merely breaking a law, then we will have a hard time with verse 5. There, John said, "*He was manifested to take away our sins, and in Him there is no sin*" (1 John 3:5 NKJV). How can those two things be reconciled? How can we say Christians who commit a sin are guilty of lawlessness and at the same time say there is no sin when we are in Jesus Christ? We talk a lot about verse 4 and tend to skip over verse 5.

The problem is that we define sin too narrowly. God is interested in the overall choices and results; he is not making up laws to trap us. Let us go back to the Garden of Eden. The problem was not just eating the fruit. The problem at its core (a small pun) was the choice to live apart from the Creator. That choice was manifested in the act itself, but there was no bad magic in eating fruit. The sin was leaving God and choosing to live without God.

There is some truth to the idea that sins must be repented of, but I would be careful of your blanket statement. It might be interpreted that every sin for a Christian will separate us from the Lord without and unless we specifically confess and repent of that particular sin. Is it possible, or even likely, that we commit sins we are unaware of or forget to identify in a nightly prayer? Are we only saved because we specifically remember and ask forgiveness for every sin? Are we condemned in the hours or days between the act of sin and the later prayer of confession?

Again, we tend to dwell on each sin and make that the focus. In Christ, we are living in repentance and his blood is continuously washing us. Remember "*In him there is no sin.*" Does that mean there is no breaking of a rule by Christians? No. It means there is no sin because we are no longer sinners and are not in the state of sin. Forgiveness overcomes the acts of wrong we do that might lead us to choose a life apart from Jesus Christ. At the same time, we are living in a changed state, a state of repentance from sin. We continually walk away from anything that is not beneficial and thank God for his forgiveness. Our salvation is not dependent on our perfection of avoiding sin nor is it dependent on our perfect repentance.

Ask yourself: "What does it mean that there is no sin in me? Does every sin I commit separate me from our Maker unless and until I remember it and confess it?"

VI. Falling from Grace

I want to accept that we are not condemned in Christ, and nothing can separate us from God. But doesn't Paul also say we can fall from grace? Is that true and, if so, at what point can we fall?

The answer for your questions starts with our ability to choose. Unless you live by the view that life is predetermined and we have no choice, then the fact you are a Christian means you chose God rather than not God. Does becoming a follower of God take away your ability to choose? No! We can always choose not to follow the Lord at any point in our life. Note, though, the possibility of something happening does not mean necessarily that it will happen often or that it will happen to us.

When we were told in Romans 8:38 "*nothing can separate us from God,*" that means no outside forces can overcome God's being there for us and holding on to us. Paul gave several examples of these possible interferences, all of which are part of the creation. Paul did not say we are prevented from separating ourselves. He also did not say God removes our free will. God is faithful and does not give up on us. That should give us a great deal of confidence and assurance. For those Christians who believe in the "once saved, always saved" interpretation, their assurance comes from the idea they are among the group that the Almighty has chosen, and that group cannot ever lose salvation. For those of us who believe in free will or choice, our assurance of a saved position can sometimes be more tenuous. While we believe the Lord will not let go of his end of the rope, we think that we might. In other words, our confidence in God's promises is sometimes limited by the confidence we have in ourselves. Since we have walked away from the Lord in the past, might we do so again?

Any doubts on our part can be accentuated by confusion over the phrase "fall from grace." That term is a bit misleading and therein lies the rub. We think of a fall in terms of an accident. We want to trust the Father on his end, but we live in constant fear an accident on our part will leave us behind. That is because we do not fully accept that God has both the desire and the power to forgive us of all sin and guilt. We say we have no sin or guilt, but we have a hard time giving up the feeling of guilt. Problematically, if we are not guilty, then why do so many Christians still feel guilty? It is because they fear the accidents and slipups that will cause them to "fall" into the water and drown. They do not doubt the Lord, nor do they doubt their intentions. Instead, they doubt their ability to stick to their plan.

In other words, those who continue to live with guilt and the fear of failure are likely still relying on their own efforts to obtain righteousness before the Lord. They are not trusting in the power and the grace of the blood of Jesus Christ. Rather, they are trusting in their perfection and their ability to avoid mistakes. When Paul addressed the people in Galatia and spoke of falling from grace, he was talking to those who had known God but were turning back by trying to keep the whole law (Galatians 4:9). And those same people were putting added law requirements on others as well. Specifically, they were requiring submission to circumcision before salvation could happen. Paul said, *"For if you are trying to make yourselves right with God by keeping the law, you have been cut off from Christ! You have fallen away from God's grace"* (Galatians 5:4 NLT). We think following the law and the rules is a good thing. It usually is, but it becomes a problem when we use our compliance as a path to God in place of Jesus Christ. That is why Paul said Christians had been set free, but some chose to return to slavery. By requiring circumcision, they were, in fact, saying that Jesus and his death really did not have the power to save them. In the same way, by living in fear that our future sins or mistakes will overcome us, we are not trusting in the Savior's forgiveness and grace.

When Paul said we can fall from grace, he emphasized that such a condition was equivalent to alienation from Christ. We can only be detached from Jesus Christ when we choose to do that. Separation from the Lord does not come through a mistake or a sin on our part. We can only leave God when we choose to leave, either through direct confrontation or through our actions. Conversely, our Father will never leave us. We do not need to fear or agonize over the fact that some people have chosen to leave the Spirit and therefore have rejected grace. That is not, however, our choice nor our destiny.

The second question has to do with when someone might fall from grace. It helps perhaps to focus again on the concept of free will. There are two basic ways I can get out of my relationship with, say, Smith. I can make the choice to terminate the relationship and even declare that decision to Smith. Or, I can simply quit participating socially with Smith, not returning calls, giving excuses, etc. The effect is the same in both cases--a broken relationship. The "point" at which a relationship ceases is the decision by at least one of the parties. When my decision is not well-communicated, Smith may not get the point at first and it may seem like there is no specific point of separation. For me, the other party, the point of broken relationship is the decision. Of course, God does not sit around trying to wonder when someone does not show up for a while. He knows our heart so knows the option we choose and the timing of that choice. The good news is that we should not worry about some possible future choice, unless we are planning to make that choice now. It is not worth any anxiety for a Christian who cannot even imagine a life apart from the Lord. God will not leave us, and we have no desire or thought of leaving him. Hence the assurance and confidence.

If we are not careful, we deny ourselves the freedom of living in today because we fear we might leave God in the future. Our emphasis on the possibility of choosing not God indicates a reliance on ourselves for our own salvation instead of the trust we are saved. We have often been hesitant to say, "I am saved," precisely because we worry our future actions and choices will disqualify us somehow. That shows we think our future actions and goodness will save us in the end. It is interesting Paul said, "*Neither the present nor the future will separate us from God*" (Romans 8:38 NIV). We do not have to worry about the future, because God is not going to let the future separate us. We cannot let the future do that either, by our continued anxiety. We absolutely do not need to worry that the Savior will give up on us. Dwelling on our own rejection of God at some future date is a fool's errand. Certainly, Christians do sometimes hang on to feelings of guilt from past sins, despite our constant assurance that the Father has fully forgiven and forgotten them. However, Christians also harbor equally strong feelings of anxiety over unrealized future sins or choices. We need to think in terms of being saved today instead of thinking we will be saved in the future only if we do not mess up.

Ask yourself: "Do I let the future control me? Am I confident in God's desire and power to forgive all my sins today, or am I anxious about possibly rejecting God tomorrow?"

VII. Body Blows

Doesn't 1 Cor. 9:27 sounds a lot like a "struggle" in which Paul is presently and [at least to some degree] engaged?

I may miss your question, but I do not see this as related that much to what I am addressing. My claim is that God's forgiveness and salvation are complete and that we longer need to struggle daily with sin as if sin is about to overcome us at any minute. This passage is not really addressing Paul's salvation or any battle or struggle with sin. Rather, he discussed his preaching of the Gospel and what he must do to reach people. He picked up on the idea of slavery to show to what extent he would go to be successful. In verse 19 he said he would become a slave to everyone in order to win them to Christ. What does it mean to be a slave? It involves in some respect giving up control or freedom. Here, Paul gave up his freedom in Christ in order to live under some of the restrictions that the Jews or the Greeks lived under. He was willing to take on some duties of the law when he was around those who follow the law meticulously. Again, he was not talking at all about his salvation or his wanting to avoid sin. In the 19-23 section sin is not even mentioned.

Paul did like to mix metaphors, so he threw in the idea of training. However, he was still talking about preaching the gospel and did not leave the slavery idea altogether. He said, "*I strike a blow to my body and make it my slave so that after I have preached to others, I myself will not be disqualified for the prize*" (1 Corinthians 9:27 NIV). How was he becoming a slave? He was giving up his time and freedom to train hard. This was still tied to his preaching, and he claimed again to make himself a slave as he did before. He did not want to miss the prize. What is the prize? We tend to think that is salvation or heaven, but again there is nothing here in this passage about those things. Why did he want to make himself a slave in verse 19? To win as many as possible. Why did he want to make himself a slave in verse 27? It was so he would not be disqualified for the prize. Logic would say these two goals are the same thing or very related. He did not want to lose the prize of winning as many as possible. The prize was not his personal salvation, his entering heaven, or freedom from sin. The prize referred to the sharing of the gospel and the bringing of people to Jesus Christ. Training your body to preach and struggling with sin may seem to sound alike but really are two different things.

There are many struggles in life. I never said there were not situations of pain, evil, or sin that we encounter. My contention is that when we become Christians, our sins are forgiven completely, and all guilt is removed. Therefore, we no longer need to struggle with guilt or the feelings of guilt. We no longer need to struggle with trying to be perfect or to overcome sin in order to be saved at some point in the future. We no longer need to conquer sin because the Lord has conquered the power and negative effects of sin.

Ask yourself: "Why do I feel like life is a constant struggle with sin? Is it because I think our Heavenly Father is disappointed with me when I sin? Am I still trying to improve myself to gain God's approval?"

VIII. Choice of Torment or Not

There simply can be no eternal conscious torment, and certainly nobody who would choose it!! Do you agree?

While the book is not primarily on heaven and hell, I did discuss them. We always must be careful to avoid too strong of a position on heaven and hell for two reasons. One, while the Bible does speak of heaven and hell, we must admit that we do not have a lot of details. I am sure most Christians would like to know more. Two, because relatively little is said, opinions therefore vary considerably among Christians. I take three positions about hell. First, hell is either a synonym for being in the not God state or else closely tied to that. Anyone who is said to be in hell is one separated from God. Second, hell is not a physical place and does not have associated attributes like literal fire or gates. However, the state of hell is very unpleasant and bad indeed because it is the state of being away from the Lord and his wonderful qualities. Third, all of us have the choice to select God or not God so therefore have the choice to select heaven or hell.

The criticism noted at the beginning says there cannot be an eternal conscious torment. I will say that although hell may not be a physical lake of fire it could be described as intense suffering. The Bible uses the term torment. What

Epilogue: Yes...But

better way to describe what it is like to be out of the presence of Yahweh? Fire, darkness, gnashing of teeth all suggest anguish or torment. I am not sure what the critic means by "conscious" torment. It seems to me that would be the only kind. Would not unconscious suffering be no suffering at all?

Now, is there "eternal" torment? Without going into verses that might deal with that, I would say that the torment of separation from God will last as long as there are people separated from God. Will a time come when all people will be saved regardless of their choice? I know some Christians do advocate a Universal Salvation. I did not argue for or against that in the book, but I am not yet convinced that the Lord will override our choice to not be with him. Do we have choice? Is our choice only limited to what God wants?

That brings us to the other point asserted: "nobody would choose this eternal conscious torment." It does perplex Christians as to why anyone might choose hell over heaven. In the same way, we are baffled as to why there is a choice of God over not God. The choice is the same. To certify that nobody would choose torment is to say nobody would choose to be separated from God. However, the Bible seems clear that people, and a fair amount of them, do choose not to be with the Creator. To deny that is to take the position that either God does not allow us a choice at all or that at some point God will override our negative choice. The alternative view is that, while we may have choice and make bad choices on earth, when we come face to face with God every single person will change their mind and choose God. I have to say that any of these positions are hard to support biblically. For example, the parable of Lazarus seems to indicate that the

Father provides everything we need to make sensible choices while we are on earth. Christians who say that any choice of opposing God here on earth will be reversed at judgment are basically saying that God does not give us adequate tools on earth to make the right choice. It is a puzzle people prefer the state of sin and hell over the state of God and love. Remarkably it does happen, does it not?

Ask yourself: "Does the Lord allow me to choose whether I want to be with him or not, or is that predetermined by him?"

IX. Struggles with Sin

Your argument that Paul's present tense language, describing his battle with sin in Romans 7:18-20, is actually a past tense literary device speaking of his pre-conversion identity, is a step I have yet to find justification for from other reliable scholars and sources. Isn't it a reality that we still must wrestle and struggle with sin and a sin nature?

You are correct that Paul spoke of a struggle in the present tense in the second half of Romans 7. If one only reads the immediate verses around the struggle part found there, then it surely does seem to point to some type of struggle he was having as a Christian. However, a few verses later he again used the present tense to say that now there is no condemnation in Christ Jesus. He further said he has been set free from the law of sin and death (a past event in his life), so therefore not presently in sin. Did sin dwell in Paul as a Christian or was he free from sin? We have three choices to interpret this apparent verb-tense dilemma: A. Paul was struggling with sin within as a Christian and was not presently free from sin, B. Paul was presently struggling with sin within, but at the same time was free from sin or, C. Paul was not presently struggling with sin within and was presently free from sin. Every choice has a tense problem.

All Christians reject A, because we know both Paul and we have been saved and set free from sin through the blood of Jesus Christ. That is a truth central to our faith. Therefore, we are left with either B or C as an understanding for what Paul was trying to say in Romans.

B is a common interpretation, because many Christians believe we still must wrestle and struggle with sin and a sin nature, despite the fact we have been saved from sin. Paul did say, "*With the mind I myself serve the law of God, but with the flesh the law of sin*" (Romans 7:25 NKJV). That seems to seal the deal for interpretation B. Or does it? Notice Paul again references the flesh or sinful nature, as some like to translate. Those who choose B as the correct interpretation see Christians as having a dual persona. They think our mind or spiritual half has been saved and the flesh or human half is either sinful or, at least, has sinful tendencies. The flesh creates an internal battle as it tries to overpower our good side. Is that what Paul said? Did he mean Christians live their lives with a sinful nature as you and others have suggested?

The answer is in the next chapter. Paul said, in the presence tense, we, "*do not walk according to the flesh but according to the Spirit*" and emphasized that "*those who are in the flesh cannot please God.*" He continued, "*You are not in the flesh but in the Spirit*" (Romans 8:4, 8-9 NKJV). Are Christians presently both in the flesh (sinful nature) and in the Spirit? Absolutely not! Paul was clear Christians are not in the flesh, which is hostile to the Lord God. Notice how he confirmed this earlier in chapter 7: "<u>When we were in the flesh</u>, the sinful passions which were aroused by the law were at work in our members to bear fruit to death. But NOW we have been delivered from the law, having died to what we were held by, so that <u>we should serve in the newness of the Spirit</u> and not in the oldness of the letter" (Romans 7:5-6 NKJV Underlining and capitalization mine). In these verses, Paul uses the past tense to say our life in the flesh is gone. He and all Christians are in the Spirit which leaves no room for any flesh or sinful nature. Then what did Paul mean when he said he served the law of sin with his flesh? What did he mean when he referenced his struggle in the flesh where nothing good dwells? He could only be referring to the time and state in which he was in the flesh before he was in the Spirit. We can get side-tracked with verb tenses and metaphors. Flesh is a metaphor for our prior unspiritual state. It is not a metaphor for a sinful body currently trying to hold our spiritual soul captive and causing us to be wretched.

If taken out of context, it might sound like Paul is struggling in his current Christian life. However, he plainly tells us that his struggle takes place at a time when he is sold under sin (Romans 7:14) and living in sin (Romans 7:20). In fact, the struggle he describes is a breakdown of what he means by being a slave. Everyone knows that Paul is not a slave to sin at the time he is writing as a fellow Christian. The present tense for being a slave and struggling with sin refers to his pre-Christian life. Later in the same chapter, he asks, "*Who will free me from this life that is dominated by sin and death*" (Romans 7:24 NLT)? Paul joyfully replies with the obvious, "*The answer, thank God, is that Jesus Christ can and does*" (Romans 7:25 MSG). He is not saying that he is now in sin and Jesus Christ will, at some time in his future, free him. Rather, he is saying that Jesus Christ can free him now and is freeing him now from sin.

One verse later he clarifies Christians are not slaves to sin. This is because we have moved into Jesus Christ and out of the sinful state. "*NOW there is no condemnation for those who belong to Christ Jesus*" (Romans 8:1 NLT, Emphasis added). We are no longer in the struggle to be free of sin since we entered a different fellowship with Christ. "*You are not controlled by your sinful nature. You are controlled by the Spirit if you have the Spirit of God living in you*" (Romans 8:9 NLT, Underlining mine). Since the blood frees us from sin, we are no longer controlled by sin. Paul did have a current struggle with sin, although he did when he was a slave to sin and living in sin.

To choose the B option, one has to say that our Maker is not able to overcome our sinful nature here on earth. I just cannot accept that. Paul was emphatic that we have been set free from the law of sin and death and are no longer slaves. How can we be set free, when we must struggle continually with sin and a sinful nature? I do not see how some scholars and sources can reconcile how we can be in the Spirit and free from sin while still being under sin and the power of sin. It does not make sense. I know some do not agree with my take on the present tense of a struggle in Romans 7. On the other hand, how do we interpret the fact that, in chapter 8, Paul uses the present tense to say we are not in the flesh? What did Paul mean when he used the past tense in chapter 7 to say we were in the flesh but are now (present tense) in the spirit? Choice B says we are still in the flesh and the sin nature. Only Choice C rightfully acknowledges Jesus Christ has overcome the flesh or sinful nature and that we are not controlled in any way by it.

Ask yourself: "Am I free from sin or am I still a slave to sin? Am I in the Spirit or am I in the flesh (sinful nature)? Does the Holy One really require us to live in a sinful body constantly causing battle with our spiritual selves?"

X. God's Rules vs Man's Rules

What are the criteria one must use to ascertain the difference between human made rules and God's rules?

My opinion is the Bible is not always clear in this area. There is some ambiguity. We must follow every law, or we must not? That is not easy to answer. Jesus did not follow every law and yet said not one bit of the law will disappear! How clear is that? In the book I did not give a list (criteria) for when we must do one thing and not the other although we discussed he need to work from the godly principles. I believe that sometimes the solution is fuzzy and is not always consistent from time to time or people to people. Certainly, none of us want to say anything goes, but if we are honest, we must admit that Christians do pick and choose and modify rules and laws. I do not require animal sacrifice and I do not require circumcision. When did God say those requirements went away?

Epilogue: Yes...But

Let me address what I think is one problem. Because there is not always a set stated answer, we want to come up with a way to determine one. For some of us, we have decided that the solution lies in knowing what God's laws are and what humans' laws are. To ask about the criteria related to ascertaining the difference, we may be asking the wrong question. We are assuming, perhaps, that deciding what is God's law and what is man's law is the key. The point I was trying to make was that there is precisely not always a list or criteria for that either. Asking such a question reduces what we want to have in relationship down to following the right list. There is, however, no right list of God's rules. The Bible nowhere gives us a complete list of rules and laws, nor does it give us always immutable laws. We must make decisions not just on what the Lord said or did not say. Deciding everything on the basis of God's law verses man's laws works sometimes, but often (or at times) does not do enough. The Jews got in trouble all the time with Jesus over this. We often say that they had the right idea, but just did not have it all together. They simply missed the right list. We all think we know what that list is. We do not. We sometimes try to say that the Creator had old rules that did not work, so he gave us new rules in the New Testament. Honestly though, the New Testament does not give a list of rules. It does not tell us always how to decide what are man's laws and what are God's laws. We then create ways like "Speak where the Bible speaks and be silent where the Bible is silent," "Apostolic example equals direct command," or "In matters of faith unity and in matters of opinion liberty." Those have some value but are not from Jesus. They are from Christians trying to get the list right-to be able to have set answers.

However, we keep arguing over what is faith and what is opinion. You and I probably do not even fully agree on the list. And I know we would have opinions on what are opinions. What I am saying is that we need to work more on the principles and less on laws themselves. It is not about trying all the time to interpret what rules God may or may not have given us. It is not about the difference between human made rules and God's rules. It is about how we can go beyond all rules to be the kind of person we were created to be. Jesus and Paul are clear that we are not bound by law, but unhappily we want to keep binding ourselves. Rules are primarily for the ignorant and those who do not want to follow Yahweh. That is what Paul said. He also said, *"If a living relationship with God could come by rule-keeping, then Christ died unnecessarily"* (Galatians 2:21 MSG). That is a strong statement for the law-and-order crowd.

Ask yourself: "Where is the complete list of God's laws found in the New Testament? If it is only about determining which rule is God-made and which is man-made, why do we have so much disagreement?"

XI. Hyper-Grace

Aren't you just teaching hyper-grace?

No, I am not, if "hyper-grace" is defined as a new, extra-biblical heresy. Yes, I am, if "hyper-grace" is a human attempt to describe the richness and power of God's grace that is beyond what some of us imagine. We love to create labels for those with whom we disagree. When we create names for others, we feel we do not need to support our views with only facts. "Hyper-grace" is a label applied to any teaching that supposedly places an extreme emphasis on grace. The accusation says proponents of hyper-grace neglect repentance, confession, and holiness, even to the point of saying those things are unnecessary for our salvation and relationship with our Father. So-called critics of hyper-grace accuse their opponents of saying people or Christians are not responsible for our sins.

Without trying to step into the debate over hyper-grace, let me say the book is primarily on forgiveness so there is an admitted focus on grace as intimately connected to God's love and forgiveness. However, I am clear that repentance and confession are huge and necessary parts of our choice of God. Absolutely, people are responsible for their own choices, including the choice of turning from sin and accepting God or staying in sin and choosing not God.

I claim to be neither a defender nor opponent of the so-called hyper-grace teaching. I certainly do not wish to take sides in the labelling and accusations. There are a couple of things that are attributed to "hyper-grace" teachings that I do touch upon in the book and might make me seem to be an advocate, which I am not.

One charge made is that hyper-grace teachers erroneously say the Lord forgives one's future sins the same way he forgives one's past sins. I believe that the Lord can and does forgive past and future sins. All forgiveness of our sins comes about because of the Lord God sending the Son to die for our sins. There are not two kinds of forgiveness from God, because all forgiveness is complete. The Lord Jesus

Christ only had to die once and did not need to keep dying over and over. His was a one-time sacrifice that covers all our sins. That must apply to more than just past sins.

A second accusation is that hyper-grace theory denies progressive sanctification (the idea that believers, with the help of the Holy Spirit, go through a process that gradually separates them from the evil of the world to be more and more like Christ). Again, I must say that salvation is complete and is not gradual. We are not partially saved upon our faith and repentance, with the hope or expectation of becoming more saved later. One is as saved upon arising from baptism as he or she will be at death. Christians are not in varying degrees of being saved, you more than me or vice versa.

It is commonly taught that redemption has two parts, salvation and sanctification. We are saved when we repent and call on the name of the Lord, but then we go through a life of sanctification. In other words, salvation is viewed as a onetime event and sanctification as a lifelong event. The Bible does not make that distinction. We are saved and sanctified fully at the same time and those cover us throughout life. *"You were washed, you were sanctified, you were justified in the name of the Lord Jesus Christ and by the Spirit of our God"* (1 Corinthians 6:11 NIV). Those things continue in us, but there is no incomplete, progressive process of sanctification.

Ask yourself: "Do I find myself, like Jonah, arguing against too much grace or too much forgiveness on the part of Yahweh?"

XII, Confession of Sins

How do you fit I Jn. 1:5-10 into your reasoning?

John said, "*If we claim to be without sin, we deceive ourselves and the truth is not in us...If we claim we have not sinned, we make him out to be a liar and his word is not in us*" (1 John 1:8, 10 NIV). In the middle of that section, he added, "*If we confess our sins, he is faithful and just and will forgive us our sins and purify us from all unrighteousness*" (1 John 1:9 NIV). Does John say Christians are in sin? Some say that he implies it using the theoretical "we." This verse is also used to support the argument that Christians who sin need to confess to each other. Maybe they do need such mutual confession, but John is not making that point at all in this section. He is not talking about Christians who sin and then need to confess. Rather, he refers to the people who are still in sin but deny the existence of sin altogether.

In this passage, John contrasts two kinds of people. One group of people are the ones who say they have no sin and, therefore, do not need Christ. The other group is made up of those who admitted that they have sinned, recognized they were separated from God, and now have turned to God. Consider the two groups:

1. Those who claim they have no sins/deny ("if we" Verses 8 and 10. Deceiving themselves. Not having truth. Making God a liar. Not having God's word in them.)

2. Those who admit/confess they have sins ("if we" Verse 9. Receiving forgiveness. Being purified from unrighteousness.)

Does group 1 refer to Christians who do not confess and group 2 refers to Christians who do confess? No. Group 1 are non-Christians who deny sin and therefore still have a need for a savior. The Group 1 descriptions can in no way apply to Christians. John did not consider himself or other Christians as not having truth, not having God's word, and making God a liar. Group 2, on the other hand, refers to Christians who have admitted sin and accepted Jesus Christ as savior.

I will point out the light/darkness metaphor just as John does in this section. Compare this secondary grouping to the one above:

A. Those who claim fellowship with him but walk in darkness ("if we" Verse 6. Lying. Not living in truth.)

B. Those who walk in the light ("if we" Verse 7. Fellowshipping with each other. Being purified from all sin.)

In verses 6-7, John uses the "we" not as inclusive of his Christian readers and him, but the "we" is inclusive of everyone in a supposed group. Another way to do that is to use the term "one." We could as easily refer to a supposed person thusly, "One might do this, or one might do that." Notice John says, "if we walk in the darkness" and then, conversely, "if we walk in the light." He certainly is not saying that he and his Christian readers are walking in darkness and light at the same time, but rather he is alluding to the supposed "anyone" who does one or the supposed "anyone" who does the other. Those in darkness are liars and not in truth while those in the light are purified from sin. Then in verses 8 and 10 he picks up the same contrast. Those who claim to never have sinned are the ones deceiving themselves and not having the truth. It is plain these are the same as the ones in verse 6, i.e., the ones who are in the darkness. In contrast to the ones in darkness are those who confess their sins and are purified from unrighteousness. Again, these confessors in verse 9 are the same as the ones in verse 7, the ones purified from sins and walking in the light. John is not saying in chapter 1 that Christians are in sin and in chapter 3 they are not in sin. Rather, in both chapters, he is affirming those outside of Jesus Christ are sinners and those in Jesus Christ are not sinners.

People who argue that this passage teaches Christians are in sin key in on John saying "we." John never says we Christians deny sin and walk in darkness. He did say if we do deny sin exists and we do walk in darkness, then we are lying, not living in truth, deceiving ourselves, and making God a liar. On the other hand, he says if we do admit sins and walk in the light, we are receiving forgiveness, being purified from sins, and fellowshipping with each other. Which group do you think Christians are in? I am betting on the latter.

In summary, those who claimed to be without sin and therefore to have no need for Jesus Christ were liars and deceivers. John was in no way saying Christians need to confess up and admit they are sinners. Instead, he says that Christians, in contrast to the imposters, had already admitted they were sinners and therefore needed Jesus Christ. Because of that, they had accepted Christ and forgiveness of those sins.

John confirms what we have been saying: We are not sinners because our sins are being forgiven.

Ask yourself: "Are Christians people who deceive themselves and make the Lord a liar, or are they people who have been forgiven, have been purified from unrighteousness, and walk in the light? Simply, are Christians righteous, or are they sinners?"

XIII. Satan and His Power

You say, "Sin is not an outside force of evil that causes us to do things against our will." Sometimes you hear people really focus on how Satan tempts us. Personally, I don't think I need any help with temptation. I provide enough of it on my own. Do you cover anything about the role of Satan in your book?

Erased does not cover Satan in depth, but you bring up some interesting thoughts. When we discuss the role of Satan in our lives, we quickly see that it is connected intimately with sin. There are several things we should note.

Satan is not God nor is he equal to God in any respect. He is a created being just as we are and is completely subject to the Almighty. He will never defeat God. God has allowed him the freedom to choose in the much the same way we have choice. It is that choice that helps us define sin, because sin is what can and does separate us from God. You are correct that sin exists because of our decisions which are sometimes influenced by the Devil. However, Satan is not the cause nor originator of sin. He is a promoter of sin and separation. Satan's primary work is to pry us from the desired relationship with the Lord. He does that through persuasion and enticement founded on deceit, because he is the father of lies. Any power he has is centered in his abilities to encourage people to leave God. He has no power over humans beyond that.

Notice in the garden, Satan used lies and persuasion to encourage Adam and Eve to leave the Creator. He did not and could not cause them to sin against their will. Their sin resulted from their decision. Satan cannot control humans. Adam and Eve could have resisted by making the right choice. There is no evil force or dark side that can take over people. Evil is not a living force that haunts or controls us. Evil and sin result when we choose to forsake God and when we choose not to act in his image. We cannot avoid our responsibilities merely by saying, "The Devil made me do it."

When we talk about any potential power of Satan, we are talking about his influence in the world. When we choose God and accept salvation and forgiveness through the blood of Jesus Christ, sin and Satan no longer have any power over us. Satan cannot defeat us because we now live in the Spirit. There is nothing (death, powers, demons, or Satan) that can separate us from the Lord. We are promised that. Because he has no power to separate, Satan has absolutely no authority over those of us in Christ. It is disturbing to see Christians who continue to live in fear and anxiety about sin and Satan. Those insecurities are largely because they have not accepted fully the expanse of God's love. When we are completely forgiven and taken back into God's house, the door is closed on Satan. He is still there, working in the world but not in us. We are free from sin and Satan and, therefore, are free indeed. To continue to live in fear is to deny the awesome power of God.

Ask yourself: "How can Satan have any power over us once we are in the Spirit? Do I still fear dark powers that can control me or cause me to leave the Father?"

XIV. Obedience and Salvation

Where do you stand on God's grace for those who may believe in Him but try to enter (out of ignorance or incorrect teaching) into Christ in a way other than what the Word describes? In other words, does God's grace (forgiveness) accrue to one's benefit BEFORE obedience to his Word?

We enter or reenter a relationship with the Great I AM through our making a choice to be with him AND by choosing to live a life as he would have us live. We move out of living in sin and move into living in Jesus Christ. Faith would encompass belief and trust, exemplifying the choice we make. Repentance would memorialize the choice and would involve the move from sin to Spirit. Baptism and confession would be public demonstrations of the choice and the life change. We would not teach that baptism, faith, confession, or repentance have any magical properties. They are all part of the package of acceptance of God's mercy and our change of life.

Some of us were taught baptism, faith, confession, and repentance are steps that must be taken. We believed that Jesus brought in a new set of laws or rules that must be followed and obeyed in order for us to be saved and to get to heaven. Are we under a new set of rules? It is interesting that the New Testament never says there is a new set of laws to follow. Because we have extrapolated there is a set of laws we must follow, we love to sing "Trust and Obey, there is no other way" and to say it is necessary to "obey the gospel" in order to be saved. By obey, we nearly always mean following a set of laws. Neither of these exact phrases were uttered by our Lord Jesus Christ nor by the apostles. We came up with those phrases to describe our interpretation about rules that must be followed. Let us talk a bit about "obey."

The New Testament does discuss obedience. We are told to obey what Jesus commanded us, God, the Word of God, Jesus' word, Jesus' teaching, and even the law. What does that obedience to those things mean? What does it mean to obey the Lord God along with his word, teachings, and law? I would think those are all talking about the same thing. Obedience includes the whole process of choosing and following the Lord. What is his word and teaching for us? It is to love him and love people. Jesus said everything is summed up in those two things.

Obedience is about following God. That includes living our life like he wants, a life of love. Yes, we do follow and obey laws, but only as they relate to God and what he wants us to be. The goal is to follow the Creator, not follow rules. To obey the gospel is not about trying to follow rules exactly but is about choosing and following God. God did not say rules or laws are unimportant. Rules and laws will never go away because they spell out the specifics of the way we want to act. Jesus said not one tiny bit of the law will pass away. We will always have rules and laws, although following rules and laws does not save us. Following the Lord does. He saves us and forgives us, because we have chosen him and want to be with him. He does not extend grace because we have followed a set of rules perfectly. Perfection does not come before grace. We are not perfect before salvation nor are we perfect afterwards. Perfection through perfect law-keeping never works.

It is interesting that when Yahweh brought his people out of Egypt, they were his people. He gave them the ten commandments and other laws because they were his people. The law included the guidelines of what it meant to be followers of Yahweh. The law was not given to the people to make them followers.

Obedience means following the rules, does it not? The Bible speaks often of obeying the law. Note that obeying the law is equal to obeying God. Obeying God means following him, not just a list of rules. How do we know that? Jesus, in several places, showed we follow the greater principles of love, justice, mercy, etc. and any rules are ways to point to those things. Let us look at two passages to show obedience is not defined as rule keeping but rather as following the Lord. Paul said, "*So then, if those who are not circumcised keep the law's requirements, will they not be regarded as though they were circumcised*" (Romans 2:24 NIV)? This is an interesting verse. Paul says if we follow the law of God, even though we are not circumcised, we are counted as if we kept the entire law. Following the law, according to Paul is NOT about following every law. It is about following God and his principles. Samuel affirmed this when he said, "*Behold, to obey is better than sacrifice, and to heed [is better] than the fat of rams*" (1 Samuel 15:22 NIV). Sacrifices and circumcision were not only God-given laws, but they were core laws. Yet we are told that obedience is bigger than keeping the laws of sacrifice and circumcision. Is it also possible that obedience to the Almighty is bigger than a rule like baptism? Obedience does not mean keeping every single law, even every God-given law. We can be said to obey God and obey his law, even if we do not keep every law. No one keeps every law perfectly.

However, like many Christians, we were taught and maybe still believe that we must be perfect to win the favor of our Father. We believe perfection means following a list of rules or laws perfectly. Interestingly, the Bible never says we must be perfect. Jesus was clear, along with Samuel and Paul, that perfection in keeping rules is not the goal.

Your question asks whether grace applies before salvation or only after. I would have to say that God loves us and wants us to be with him for our entire lives. His love does not start at conversion. Grace was offered before salvation and any extension of grace is not conditional upon our salvation. We might believe the Lord does not demand perfection for the period of our Christian lives. Are we prepared to say he does demand perfection as we "enter" the Christian life? I would be hard-pressed to make that claim. Remember that forgiveness covers our entire life of sin and mistakes. It is not limited in coverage only to sins and imperfections committed after our first acceptance of God.

We must be careful about using rules and laws, even God's law, as a barrier to salvation. In Galatians 5:2-12, Paul was dealing with people who wanted a God-given law, circumcision, as a requirement for salvation. Paul said he hoped they mutilate themselves. Pretty tough language! Might we have a problem if we also require a certain rule be followed before a person becomes a Christian? Something to think about. We probably need to be reticent in saying the Lord requires perfect law-keeping in order to become a Christian but does not require perfect law-keeping to remain a Christian. When we think salvation comes from perfectly keeping every single rule then we kill ourselves with what-ifs and details, like the Pharisees. We start to think we have to act perfectly and believe perfectly. I did not have perfect beliefs when I was saved. That is okay, because God forgives all imperfections and all sins for my entire life. I do not have perfect beliefs and actions now, but God forgives me.

Are we saying the Lord God loves all people and that all people will be saved? No, although he does love all people. We must make the choice to accept his love and to participate in his love. We can refuse to accept his grace and we can refuse to live lives in the Spirit. If we do choose him and desire to live life with him, then God will forgive all our sins, mistakes, and imperfections for our entire lives. He has never required perfection.

Ask yourself: "Does God's forgiveness cover errors in beliefs? Am I 100% correct in my beliefs?"

XV. Chief Sinner

Doesn't Paul say he was the number one sinner and therefore imply we are all sinners?

Epilogue: Yes...But

According to some translations, Paul said, "*Christ Jesus came into the world to save sinners—of whom I am the worst. But for that very reason I was shown mercy so that in me, the worst of sinners, Christ Jesus might display his immense patience as an example for those who would believe in him and receive eternal life*" (1 Timothy 1:15-16 NIV). Interestingly, Paul never used the word "worst." The English word "worst", as used by the NIV twice in this passage, is not in the Greek. The Greek word Paul used was "protos" which means first. From the word "protos" we get words such as "prototype," which is an original or first design. In English as in Greek, first can mean first in time, but it can also mean first in rank.

In the New Testament, sometimes "protos" can be used in the sense of "most important" or "most prominent" as we might think of someone who is in first place. For example, Jesus said, "*The most important ["protos"] commandment is this: 'Listen, O Israel! The Lord our God is the one and only Lord*'" (Mark 12:29 NLT Brackets mine). He used "protos," translated here as most important. Note, however, "protos" never in the Bible means worst as translated by the NIV in 1 Timothy. I suppose the NIV translators were thinking "best sinner" would not do justice to what they were thinking! Why would Paul want to make a point that he was the "most important" or "most prominent" sinner? Did he or the readers really think Paul was somehow in worse shape than anyone else? Hardly. As we have repeatedly shown, being a sinner has nothing to do with degrees of sin but rather has to do with the state a person is in. There is nothing here in the 1 Timothy passage that suggests Paul's degree of sinfulness served as a point to be made. Perhaps people like to think that if the Almighty could forgive Paul's awful sins, he should be able to forgive our less obnoxious ones!

Most always, "protos" is used by Paul and other New Testament writers to mean first in time. For example, in chapter 2, Paul said, *"For God made Adam first ["protos"], and afterward he made Eve"* (1 Timothy 2:13 NLT Brackets mine). Is it possible in chapter 1 Paul also used "protos" as first in time instead of first in rank? Likely. Let us start with his second use of the word (albeit in a different grammar case, namely, "proto") in our passage. The literal Greek phrase in verse 16 would be rendered "in me first." That reading would mean Paul said, "In me first, I was shown mercy." Paul was not so much interested in making a point about sin as he was in making a point about salvation and the transition from sin. He went on to explain why that was important to the readers. He reasoned he was first shown mercy to serve as a pattern or example to those of readers who were coming to believe in Christ Jesus and who wanted to receive eternal life. Could we then say Paul was the redemption protype for his readers? I believe so, which makes more sense than trying to translate "in me first" as "in me, the worst of sinners." The NIV should get kudos for trying to be consistent, but it forces them, in verse 16, to employ a dubious translation.

Some other versions, recognizing that it makes more sense for verse 16 to mean first in time rather than first in rank, translate that verse accordingly. However, those same translators inexplicably still want to keep verse 15 as first in rank. They force themselves into a consistency problem. Their attempts look like this: *"Christ Jesus came into the world to save sinners, of whom I am chief ["protos"].*

Epilogue: Yes...But

However, for this reason I obtained mercy, that in me first ["proto"] Jesus Christ might show all longsuffering, as a pattern to those who are going to believe on Him for everlasting life" (1 Timothy 1:15-16 NKJV Brackets mine). Granted, while Biblical writers did engage in wordplay at times, it seems to me verses 15 and 16 are very interlocked in meaning and that there is no reason to suppose Paul is trying to convey two different thoughts. The most reasonable conclusion then is Paul uses "protos" in both verses in the same way, that of first in time.

Thus, a reading that makes the most sense, is consistent in treatment, and happens to square well with our general assertion that Christians are not sinners would be something like: "*This is a faithful saying and worthy of acceptation by all, that Christ Jesus came into the world to save sinners, of whom I am first ["protos"]. But for this cause I was received unto mercy that in me first ["proto"], Jesus Christ might show forth all clemency, for an example to those who should hereafter believe in him for eternal life*" (1 Timothy 1:15-16 JUB Brackets mine). These verses are not mainly about sin and certainly are not discussing at all how bad Paul's sins were. Rather, they are focused on salvation and mercy. He is not comparing his sin with the readers but, instead, is focused on their common salvation. The example to be followed was Paul's salvation and was not Paul's sin. In verse 16 Paul is obviously using "protos" to say he was first shown mercy in order to be a pattern for those who followed.

This idea that Paul had changed although he was formerly a sinner becomes a strong incentive for others. It also fits well with the greater context. Go up to verse 13 where

Paul says, *"Even though I was once [Greek "proteron"] a blasphemer and a persecutor and a violent man, I was shown mercy"* (1 Timothy 1:13 NIV Brackets mine). "Proteron" is similar to "protos" as it can refer to first in time or first in rank. Here in verse 13, it is obviously referring to first in time. If verses 13 and 16 use "proteron" and "proto" to refer to his earlier pre-Christian life of sin, it follows then that "protos" in verse 15 also refers to first in time. Why would Paul use "protos" two different ways in the same passage as a few translations try to do?

In verse 13, Paul was talking about two different states. One was the state of blasphemy, persecution, and violence. The other state was the state of mercy. These two different states were separated in time. One was the former life, and one is the present life. Notice how Paul separates in time by saying "I once was in" the first state when "I acted in ignorance and unbelief." (past tenses).

The present life is one of mercy. This present life of mercy is the point of the whole passage. He was making a contrast, as does the rest of the Bible, between the old life and the new life. Notice how well this fits with verses 15-16, when he continued the present mercy theme. Paul did talk about first being a sinner or, as some prefer, the foremost sinner. Either way, this being a sinner is referencing which state? The state of blasphemy, persecution, and violence, or the state of mercy? We do not have to guess, because in verse 16 Paul clearly said, "I was shown mercy." That demonstrates well that the state of being a sinner was a past state or former state, now changed because he WAS SHOWN mercy. It is neither he "will be shown mercy," nor he "was shown mercy but he is still in the state of being a sinner." Paul moved from being a sinner (blasphemer, persecutor, and violent man) to being in the state of having received mercy, i.e., saved.

In some translations it does appear that Paul, a baptized Christian, claimed to still be a sinner, and the worse sinner to boot. As we have shown, that does not make sense. Do we want to argue that Paul remained the number one sinner? Do we want to argue that God did not change him? Do believe our best appeal to the world is they can remain sinners just like Paul? I do not think so. What Paul said was my former sin and present salvation from that sin came before yours (the readers) and is indicative of the same thing that can happen for you. Like Paul, we once were sinners (blasphemers, persecutors, or whatever), but now we have received mercy and have been transformed. We have moved out of our former state of sin and are no longer classed as sinners who remain in that state.

Ask yourself: "Does the Father consider me a sinner now that I am in relationship with him? If not, why do I call myself a sinner although I have been taken out of sin and changed?"

XVI. Worthiness

Is it true we can never be worthy enough for God?

Many Christians certainly believe that and feel they are not worthy of God's love and forgiveness. You might be surprised the Bible never says we are unworthy. In fact, it seems clear that we are worthy. Paul confirms this in his letters to the Christians in Thessalonica, when he says we can live worthy lives, walk worthy of God, and be counted as worthy by God (see 1 Thessalonians 2:12; 4:12 and 2 Thessalonians 1:5, 11).

Why, then, do we constantly feel unworthy? We know the Lord is holy, perfect, and worthy to be praised. When we compare ourselves to him, it is easy to feel we come up short. That feeling of inadequacy can linger throughout our lives and leave us with a need to prove ourselves more worthy. Any time we commit sin and/or move away from the Lord we can feel alienated and at loss as to how relationship can be restored. All of us have experienced pain, anger, or resentment when someone has mistreated us or rejected us. Often, we have found it difficult to forgive in those situations and, at times, we have been unable or unwilling to reenter into fellowship with the one who has offended us. In reverse, when we believe we are the offender and have offended God, we think he will not forgive us and take us back.

We take our cue from the prodigal son in Luke 15 who thought he must return home as a slave perhaps, but certainly not as a full family member. When he first comes face to face with his father, the son adamantly declares, "I am no longer worthy of being called your son." We tend to think the story stops there. However, the story is not primarily about the son. It is about the father. That is why the story continues with a "But the father...." The son did think himself unworthy to have relationship after his choices, but the father had other ideas. The key is found at the conclusion to the parable when the father says, "Everything I have is yours." By saying that, the father has deemed the son does have value.

The word worthy is defined as "having value, worth, or merit." It is a hard concept to learn, but we need to understand value is always determined by the buyer and not by the seller. A few years ago, I decided to sell a used car and listed it for $5,000. No one called. I finally sold it for much less. Was it worth $5,000? No, despite what I thought and what I was asking. A car or anything is only worth what a buyer will pay and nothing more. If no one wanted to buy the car, it would have been worthless. Similarly, it is incorrect to say a certain painting or gemstone is priceless. An item is never priceless because someone will buy it. God is the buyer in our case, and he has decided we do have value. What are we worth to Yahweh? What price was he willing to pay? Of course, it was the ultimate price—his coming to die for us. We have value in his sight. When we say we do not or we continue to see ourselves as unworthy, we are denying the opinion of God and belittling the cost that was paid.

Ask yourself: "Can I accept that the Lord God as deemed me worthy to be with him? Do I feel like I am worthy all the time?"

XVII. Be Perfect

You said that God does not demand perfection. Aren't we told to be perfect?

Undoubtedly, you are referring to the declaration from Jesus: "*You therefore must be perfect, as your heavenly Father is perfect*" (Matthew 5:48 ESV). Does that mean without sin? Not likely. You will notice that the sins are not mentioned here. The context is about how we keep the rules or fulfill the law. The Greek word for perfect can also be translated as complete. That translation would make sense because Jesus has been referring to actions that are more inclusive than most people would require. Jesus would then be asking us to follow the Father completely rather than partially, as was being done by the listeners. Notice that Jesus has been talking about the principled law of love for neighbor. He accuses the people of trying to narrowly apply rule laws as requirements rather than taking the broader view of love. He calls them to complete or fulfill the law of love. Our model is the Lord because he proved what love really is. Jesus would never say we had to model God's total lack of sins because we cannot do that. In fact, he is not even directly referring to sin here.

Interestingly, we have a similar story when the rich young ruler visited Jesus. Jesus told him to follow the rule laws to gain eternal life. The young man said he had. Jesus, knowing they had differing views on what it meant to please God, responded, "*If you would be perfect, go, sell what you possess and give to the poor, and you will have treasure in heaven; and come, follow me*" (Matthew 19:21 ESV). Perfection is seen as choosing the Lord through the process of following the more complete principled law of generosity and through following Jesus Christ. The context shows us the word often translated as perfection refers to completeness. This point is driven home in the way other gospel writers understood the story. Mark and Luke did not even write down the word "perfect" in this story but rather relayed Jesus' meaning this way: "*You lack one thing: go, sell all that you have and give to the poor, and you will have treasure in heaven; and come, follow me"* (Mark 10:21 ESV). Being perfect and not lacking anything are equivalent versions of what Jesus intended. The man's imperfections were clearly due to incompleteness! The young man believed that following the rule laws would gain him eternal life. He likely also believed that is all he should do. He wanted to make sure that he had not missed any of these rule laws. Jesus encouraged him to do two more things to achieve completeness in his quest: follow the superior principled law and choose Jesus Christ. Those are two things we all are called to do. Give up the old life and follow the Lord in a new life. In this story, we sometimes concentrate on the giving up of the riches, but we should also realize completeness involved following Jesus too. The young man, unhappily, did not want to choose the Lord. He apparently preferred trying to achieve eternal life on his own. That is why the real point of the story comes when Jesus responds to the disciples' astonishment. He tells them that salvation is impossible for humans to achieve on their own. With God, all things are possible.

In both incidences when Jesus mentions perfection, he is referring to completing the picture in our walk with God. For Jesus, that means moving beyond a narrow focus of trying to follow a list of rule laws and into a broader arena of acting as God would want us to act. It is not a call for us to achieve perfection through never sinning and never breaking a rule law. Nowhere in the Bible does it require us to be perfect in the sense that we never err. The good news is it does not matter. The Lord God forgives all our imperfections and anything we lack! He makes us complete or perfect by forgiving any imperfections. God makes us perfect or complete when we choose to follow him. "*With one sacrifice Christ made his people perfect forever. They are the ones who are being made holy*" (Hebrews 10:14 ERV).

Ask yourself: "Am I equating sin and imperfection? Do any of my guilt feelings result from things I fail to do?"

XVIII. Sin that Leads to Death

I believe my Bible says there is one sin that leads to death, and we should not even bother to pray about it. I worry I may commit that sin and not be able to be forgiven. Is there a sin that leads to death and cannot be forgiven?

Let us remember that the blood of Jesus forgives us of all sin when we accept that truth and enter a relationship with God. We are told that expressly in several places and the Lord does not lie. If we say God is incapable of forgiving every sin, we deny his power and we negate the sacrifice of Jesus Christ.

Having said that, we must admit that there are a few places in the Bible which might cause us to question the idea of complete forgiveness. One of them is this: "*If you see any brother or sister commit a sin that does not lead to death, you should pray and God will give them life. I refer to those whose sin does not lead to death. There is a sin that leads to death. I am not saying that you should pray about that. All wrongdoing is sin, and there is sin that does not lead to death.*" (1 John 5:16-17 NIV)

In more than one place in the letter we call 1 John, John plainly said that those of us in Christ do not sin and cannot sin. In other places, he talked of Christians

Epilogue: Yes...But

committing sins or the possibility of Christians committing sins. How can that be?

1 John 5 will help us. Translators have muddied the waters, so we must deal with that first. We will pick on the New International Version, a generally reliable translation. Remember that translations are done by people like you and me and they must make choices of words and phrases. This passage has puzzled us. According to the NIV and many other translations, John was referring to some particularly dangerous sin that Christians need to avoid. If there is such a sin, it is unidentified in the text. We do not know what it might be and can only surmise the readers did. The context gives no clue to this mysterious sin.

However, in my opinion, the idea that Christians can commit this unforgivable sin does not compute with the idea of Christians not being in sin. Further examination will show this passage is not that hard to understand and, indeed, fits well with what John had been saying all along. Occasionally we must go to the original languages to find the correct meaning. In the Greek, oddly, there are no indefinite articles like "a" or "an". That linguistic oversight worked for the Greek speakers but does not always work well in English. We need our indefinite articles. If a Greek said, "I saw frog," then the listener would know what he or she meant even though there was no "a" before frog. We cannot be that ambiguous in English. We would have to translate the Greek phrase in English as "I saw a frog." That adding of an "a" or "an" is done thousands of times in the New Testament and it must be done for English readers.

Sometimes, though, problems can arise in translation. For example, what if the Greek said, "I saw sheep"? Now a translator cannot just add the indefinite article in English and say, "I saw a sheep" because the Greek speaker may have meant "I saw several sheep." Translators must consider the context and other factors, but sometimes they must guess about when to add articles. In our chapter 5 passage, the word "sin" is used several times and in the Greek original, there is no indefinite article. The English word "sin" is like the word "sheep." Both words can be singular or collective. Translators must make a choice. They cannot leave it untranslated. Many translations such as the NIV have chosen in our 1 John 5 case to add the indefinite article before "sin" in verse 16. Some versions even translate it as "one sin" rather than "a sin." Adding such indefinite articles or adjectives here assumes John refers to a particular sin, despite the fact he does not identify such a sin. Translating here with "a" sin or "one" sin still leaves a lot of questions and does not make much sense. It causes versions like the NIV to switch the meaning in verse 17 by leaving off the indefinite article there, which is a strange way to translate. Is it good translating to put the indefinite article in verse 16 and leave it out in the next verse? No! In fact, it is very inconsistent and problematic because it leaves us scratching our heads. Worse, it leads many Christians to live in a constant fear that they might be committing this unidentified sin that irreversibly leads to death and destruction.

In Bible translation, one of the general rules is that the simpler meaning is preferred. Here, leaving off the indefinite article in both verses makes much more sense and is the simpler translation. Notice this translation: *"Suppose you see your fellow believer sinning (sin that does not lead to eternal death). You should pray for them. Then God will give them life. I am talking about people whose sin does not lead to eternal death. There is sin that leads to death. I don't mean that you should pray about that kind of sin. Doing wrong is always sin. But there is sin that does not lead to eternal death"* (1 John 5:16-17 ERV). This is a perfectly valid translation that is simpler, more consistent, and fits in better with what John has been saying in the whole book. It implies there is sin that leads to death and sin that does not lead to death, which we know to be true. That fits smoothly into John's thought and does not force the reader into wondering why John has randomly inserted a particular unforgivable but unknown sin into his discussion.

John had spent a great deal of the book talking about the contrasts between light and darkness as well as life and death. He stayed with those themes here. John said that Christians do commit sins, but because of the life that comes from the blood, those sins do not lead to death. In that sense, Christians do not sin. There is sin that does not lead to death because we are alive, and those sins are forgiven. Conversely, sin can lead to death if we choose to leave life for death, either through a direct choice or through a refusal to live in the light. Sin is ultimately a choice we make. Christians can commit a sin (break the law) without being in sin (separated from God). Thus, John could follow up his statement that Christians do not commit sin by affirming again: *"We know that whoever is born of God does not sin; but he who has been born of God keeps himself, and the wicked one does not touch him."* (1 John 5:18 NKJV).

It is tempting in verse 18 to translate "does not sin" as "does not continue to sin" under the idea that Christians sin but do not do it continuously. That attempt to soften the meaning of John is not helpful. Honestly, if we say someone does not continue to do something, that means they stop doing it. Whether we translate using "does not continue to sin" or even "stops sinning," we get back to what John really said: "A Christian does not sin." He can say that because Christians who continue to choose God can commit sins that do not lead to separation. Remember that the definition of sin is what leads us from God. When we remain in Jesus Christ we are in the light and in the life and we are not sinners. Sin has no power over us. John often expresses this confidence we have as Christians.

Ask yourself: "Am I afraid there is an unknown sin out there that would ban me from the Lord God forever?"

XIX. Becoming Gooder

True Christian self-reflection must always be the discipline of comparing ourselves to God's desired version of us. Isn't our goal to become "gooder," if I can use that term?

We commonly tell ourselves, "We can always do better." That is often intended as a positive phrase, encouraging ourselves to bigger and greater things. The phrase, though, has a negative side that is not always so evident. To say the next time can be better implies that this time was not quite good enough. We use the phrase most often in failure or when we place second, almost always in the context that this particular attempt can and should be followed by at least one to get it right. Maybe we were somewhat happy with today's result, but the feeling is that tomorrow's result could be better and would bring a fuller happiness if it were. Of course, that could mean greater satisfaction for us or for some observer, or for both.

It can be the same with Christians. We commonly say we could do better or even be better. Is that possible? Must we be better? Specifically, do we need to be better somehow to please God more? Is it his desire for us to improve our performance from what it is today?

Before we address the "better" portion of the phrase, let us look at the "good" part. When we say we ought to be better ("gooder"), we imply we are already good. (That is not a given, because we could be saying we are bad or a failure and want to improve upon that condition by becoming good). Regardless, that leaves us with the question: Are Christians good? That answer could depend on how we define good.

The Bible is clear that there are two kinds of people, those who choose to follow the Lord and those who do not. Jesus described those categories when he said, "*He causes his sun to rise on the evil and the good, and sends rain on the righteous and the unrighteous*" (Matthew 5:45 NIV). The righteous (the good) are the followers of God, while the unrighteous (the evil) are those who do not choose God. When we choose God, we move from being evil (in sin) to being good (in the Spirit). John put it simply, "*If you are constantly doing what is good, it is because you are good, even as he is. But if you keep on sinning, it shows that you belong to Satan*" (1 John 3:7-8 TLB). Christians are good because we now are in relationship with a good Creator, the source of all goodness. Goodness is a part of the image of God in which we were created. Our actions follow our choice and work in tandem with it.

As an aside, notice that being good has to do with our choice to commune with the Lord and is not contingent on the number of "good" deeds we do. Despite the common thought, the world is not merely made up of those who do good deeds (those who are good) and those who do bad deeds (the bad). It is made up of those who choose to follow God and those who do not. Any good deeds or bad deeds reflect our choice.

Given, then, that Christians are indeed good because they are now in relationship with a good God, can they be gooder? The answer is no. We cannot be gooder, because we are already good. If we are good in God's sight, the only one that counts, how can we be better? We cannot. We are fully saved and fully connected with the Lord. We are fully good. In that respect, the Lord God is not desiring for or expecting us to be closer to him. To say that implies we are not close enough to him now. Claiming we can be gooder or better says we are not good enough today, which is a lie. We need to stop creating guilt by teaching the Lord wants us to be better or do more good deeds to merit his approval. God is happy and satisfied with us right now. I am good and doing good today because I accepted God's forgiveness and grace. I will continue to be good and do good tomorrow because I am his child. Nothing can change that unless, God forbid, I make the choice to leave him and return to sin and evil.

Ask yourself: "Is my ultimate salvation contingent on how good I am or how much I improve while I am a Christian?"

XX. All In on Sin

The Bible says that we have all sinned and none is righteous. Doesn't that suggest all people, Christians and non-Christians, are sinners?

You are referring to Paul's quote from the Old Testament: *"No one is righteous—not even one. No one is truly wise; no one is seeking God. All have turned away; all have become useless. No one does good, not a single one"* (Romans 3:10-12 NLT). We should know that this statement is right in the middle of an argument about whether Gentiles should have to become Jews and follow all Jewish laws in order to be saved. Paul opened this section by claiming all people, whether Jew or Gentile, are under the power of sin. He wanted to make the point that Jews are not exempt and that both groups are in the same boat when it comes to sin. He went on to say clearly that we have all sinned, Jews and Gentiles, but the Yahweh was for the Gentiles also and not just for the Jews. Given that, we need to be careful in saying Paul was trying to deal with the question of whether Christians today sinners are or not. However, for argument's sake, we will ignore the immediate context and address the passage as if it were speaking to this concern and addressing our individual situations.

When Paul said we all have sinned and all become useless, I do not think he was trying to say that means our present life as Christians. Instead, he referenced a former life, before we moved into relationship with the Father. Notice the rest of the quote also describes these "sinners" as people who commit murders, have venom dripping from their lips, and have no fear of God. Does that sound like an apt description for Christians? We cannot say Christians are presently sinners without also saying they are in that category of people who have no fear of God, are miserable liars, and are full of cursing. Sin is a horrible thing that separates us from the Lord. That is why the Bible uses such images as murder, venom, and misery to describe the state of sin. Christians are not in that sin condition anymore and therefore are neither living in nor controlled by those awful, hellish things that Paul described.

The quote does say, "*No one is righteous—not even one.*" Does this mean literally everyone at this moment, both followers of God and those opposed to God, are unrighteous? We must be careful. If we use the quote as proof that Christians remain sinners, then we are required to argue that there is not a single righteous person anywhere. We are saying we are all unrighteous and will remain so our entire life. The good news is that Paul did not argue that. I realize some Bibles include a heading here that says, "All People are Sinners." That heading was not placed by Paul and was not in the Bible. Unfortunately, it is that type of theology that dominates our thinking at times. We rely on the headings and not on the fine print.

Pay attention to what Paul did mean. If we go down a few verses, he said, "*Everyone has sinned; we all fall short of God's glorious standard. Yet God, in his grace, freely makes*

Epilogue: Yes...But

<u>us right in his sight.</u> *He did this through Christ Jesus when he freed us from the penalty for our sins....He makes sinners right in his sight when they believe in Jesus*" (Romans 3:23-24, 26 NLT Underling mine). Are we sinners or have we been made right by the Lord God? Paul seems clear that while we were once sinners, that has changed. We are no longer in the miserable, venomous state of sin and unrighteousness. The "yet God" is key. Paul continued, "*People are counted as righteous, not because of their work, but because of their faith in God who forgives sinners*" (Romans 4:5 NLT). Paul said the Lord considers us right through forgiveness. Christians are righteous. When he says no one is righteous, he means no one is right on their own and without the Lord. Further, when he says no one is righteous. he is not speaking of Christians who have been made right.

Ask yourself: "Am I right with God and free from sin or am I unrighteous and still in sin?"

XXI. Guilt Feelings

Aren't some guilt feelings good for us, to help motivate ourselves?

That is an interesting question. One person even recently said the thorn in the flesh was Paul's continued feelings of guilt over past sins. I understand somewhat the thinking that guilt feelings could be good for us. However, I believe that thinking might come from a misunderstanding of the nature of guilt. Guilt arises when a person does something wrong or incorrect and the action deserves punishment of some kind. When the Lord pardons us, he counts us righteous and not deserving of punishment or estrangement from him. Being declared free from sin and guilt does not mean we might not have feelings of regret or remorse for our actions. In those cases, the remorse can lead to repentance or a change in actions. The key is to understand feelings of regret or remorse are not the same as feeling of guilt. Feeling regret for sin and making a change can be good. Feeling guilty when God has taken guilt away seems to be admitting we feel the guilt is still there.

I have a hard time seeing God come and die to take away sin and guilt and then leaving us with the burden of continued shame. While the Bible does address the guilt of sins, I do not think it speaks much about the feelings of guilt. John did talk once concerning whether our hearts condemn us or not. One translation puts it like this: "*Our actions will show that we belong to the truth, so we will be confident when we stand before God. Even if we feel guilty, God is greater than our feelings, and he knows everything. Dear friends, if we don't feel guilty, we can come to God with bold confidence*" (1 John 3:19-20 NLT).

Ask yourself: "Does my Father want me to have bold confidence or continued guilt feelings?"

In Summary

I hope these discussions have been helpful for you. As noted, the answers are not about winning theological arguments on obscure passages. Rather, we are trying to understand the Lord and our relationship to him. It all gets down to how we view God. Is he loving, merciful, and kind or is he hard to please and arbitrary? Does God overlook all our sins and extend unmerited grace to us, or is he expecting us to work our way up the ladder in attempts to make him satisfied? Recently, a dear Christian acquaintance, in all sincerity, said God was narrow-minded. By that, she was referencing Jesus' words about the narrow and broad way. For her, that meant the Lord made it somewhat difficult to find him and to please him.

Here is the thing, though. Yahweh is pleased with you and me. He has honored us by counting us worthy to be his friend. Do not overthink it. Live in the "Yes" and not in the "But." Is our God narrow-minded or is he big-hearted? "*Come to me, all you who are weary and burdened, and I will give you rest. Take my yoke upon you and learn from me, for I am gentle and humble in heart, and you will find rest for our souls. For my yoke is easy and my burden is light*" (Matthew 11:28-30 NIV).

Acknowledgments

I AM THANKFUL to a long list of teachers, friends, and family who have shaped my views of God and my place in the world. Those views have been dynamic and, I believe, forever improving. It is out of that lifetime of learning this book has arisen.

I am especially grateful to all the people who directly supported me, encouraged me, and even argued with me about the book. Specifically, I wish to thank Martin Moore, Jimmy Rogers, Beverly Stanglin, Janice Stephenson, Mark Wade, and Kelly Willing for taking the time to read various drafts. It was scary to ask someone else to read and critique my work. Fortunately, this group of friends was very understanding and offered many suggestions and ideas. I truly learn best when challenged and when I must support my beliefs. Note, however, that I am solely responsible for the content, my opinions, and any errors.

About the Author

GARY L. HOLMES has always been interested in Christian theology. His formal training came at Oklahoma Christian with a BA degree in Bible and at Harding School of Theology with a Masters of Theology degree. After serving as a missionary in Brazil, Holmes had a successful career as a CPA and business broker. He has written for journals and spoken for professional groups across the United States.

Holmes lives in Texas where he is active in the Mansfield Church of Christ. He spends his time writing, enjoying five grandsons, collecting Roman coins, and occasionally whale watching.

Connect with the Author

I hope you enjoyed reading *ERASED: God's Complete Forgiveness of Sins* as much as I enjoyed writing it. Connect with me at gary@firemountainpublishing.com. Your comments, suggestions, and corrections will be taken seriously. I look forward to hearing from you!

If you enjoyed this book and found it useful, I'd be very grateful if you'd post an honest review on Amazon. Your support does matter, and it really makes a difference. Reviews and testimonials can be given at Amazon, any other site where you bought this book, or www.firemountainpublishing.com. I read all the reviews so I can get your feedback and make changes because of that feedback.

Discussion Questions

Chapter One

1) Do you ever seek out people or books that disagree with your views? What benefits might come from listening to those who have different opinions? What harm can result?
2) How would you describe righteousness?
3) It is often said all Christians struggle in sin. How would you describe what that means? Would you say the struggle is with outside forces or with something within us?
4) Has it ever bothered you that your beliefs about God or the church might have changed? How might your views of God have changed over the years?
5) Why does the term Christian sinner seem oxymoronic?
6) What do you think John means when he says that no one who lives in Jesus Christ keeps on sinning? How can we say that Christians stop sinning?

Chapter Two

1) Do Christians use a unique language? How might the language we speak and the esoteric words we use affect how we communicate with non-Christians?
2) Why do people often prefer a middle ground between God and not God? Do Christians also feel that way at times?
3) Do you agree that people who go to hell do so because of their choice? Do you think anyone will be surprised at judgment day? Why or why not?
4) Do most Christians know they are saved and know they are going to heaven? Why might that be in doubt?
5) What is meant by saying sin is a negative concept?
6) Does God require us to be good? Do you agree that many Christians think salvation is tied in some way to how good we are? What might a Christian say to make you think he or she still feels that way?
7) Do you ever feel you might need to be better? How can that sometimes be unhealthy?

Chapter Three

1) What would you say are the key things we do in our relationship with the Lord?
2) Did Jesus ever break one of God's laws? Did he ever say that we can do so?
3) Why do we follow some Old Testament laws and not others? Who decides?
4) Is it ever allowable for humans to change one of God's laws? If so, when might that be?

5) How can it be said God's laws are necessary but not always absolute?
6) Do you agree that sin is anything that separates us from the Lord or can lead to separation from the Lord? If not, how do you define sin?
7) When can something be a sin for one person but might not be for another?
8) How can it be said the Bible supplies all our answers when some specific sins are not mentioned?

Chapter Four

1) The point is made that sin is not just about breaking a law. Do you agree? Explain.
2) How would you describe what it means to be free from sin?
3) Do you believe that the first sin we commit separates us from God? Why or why not?
4) How can it be said some sins lead to death for Christians and some do not? What is the difference?
5) Do you consider yourself a sinner? Explain your thoughts.
6) Some people say a sinner is anyone who commits sins. Why is that definition inadequate for Christians?
7) Do you believe all Christians sin daily? Why or why not?
8) Why does the writer say it is not normal for Christians to struggle constantly in sins?

Chapter Five

1) Does forgiveness always involve the restoration of relationships? Give examples.
2) Is it fair to expect Christians to be the most forgiving people in the world? Do you think they are?
3) Do Christians continue to have a sinful nature? Do we continue to be predisposed to sin?
4) Do you feel there are past sins in your life that might be hard for God to forgive? Do you pray repeatedly for the forgiveness of a particular sin?
5) How can the church show forgiveness to murderers or sex offenders? What should the policies be?
6) Are you ever bothered by things you should have done but didn't? Do you feel there is more you could or should do in your Christian life? How does relate to our desire to be perfect?
7) Does it bother you that some who claim to be Christians have different beliefs from you? How can we overlook or forgive what we consider to be incorrect beliefs?

Chapter Six

1) At what point does the Lord forgive individual sins in your life?
2) What is the purpose of confession of sins? Is it necessary to repent of every sin to have forgiveness?
3) Are the requirements for salvation different between now and the Old Testament times? If so, how?

Discussion Questions

4) Do you agree that God will forgive the sins you have not yet committed?
5) Why does the writer say Christians need to be cautious in talking about a journey towards God?
6) Is it possible for Christians to leave the Lord? Explain your reasoning.
7) Will the Lord forgive a Christian who keeps committing the same sins in an addiction? Is it possible to be so addicted to sin we lose the ability to quit?

Chapter Seven

1) Why does the writer say there is no cheap or costly grace for us?
2) Do you ever feel obligated to God to do something or act a certain way? How might that relate to our view of forgiveness?
3) Is it common for Christians to see themselves as the older brother in the Parable of the Prodigal Son? Do you ever doubt the sincerity of a famous person or a renowned person who repents?
4) Are you harder on yourself than on others? Why does that happen?
5) Do we fear that leniency of rules or too much forgiveness will cause Christians to be lax? Does that fear mean we might be driven by obligation instead of love?
6) How can we accept we are completely forgiven and are no longer sinners without appearing arrogant to non-Christians?

Chapter Eight

1) Can you say confidently you feel no guilt for your sins or imperfections?
2) How do you know you are in the presence of the Almighty? What does such access allow you to do that you could not do before?
3) List and share one action you can do this week to show God's love.
4) Is there anyone in your life you have not forgiven? Do you hold a grudge against another person? Do you wish ill of anyone?
5) How does our forgiveness of others affect God's forgiveness of us?
6) Do you feel doubt is a common part of the Christian life? What do you think is the key to overcoming insecurity for you?

Scripture Index

Genesis
  3:4-6 63
Exodus
  12:5 10
  33:20 5
  34:6-7 97
Leviticus
  20:10 49
  26: 27-30 6
Numbers
  15:27-31 120
Joshua
  24:19-20 6
1 Samuel
  15:22 193
Psalm
  1:1,5 71
  14:2-3 6
  37:8 71
  85:2 85
  90:4 105
  103:3 85
  104:35 71
Proverbs
  13:6, 21 71
Isaiah
  1:28 71
  13:9 71
  33:14 71
  55:6-7 125
  59:2 21
Jeremiah
  31:33-34 157
  31:34 86
Ezekiel
  18:24 71
Hosea
  6:6 54
Joel
  2:13 92
Jonah
  4:2-3 129
Habakkuk
  1:13 5
Matthew
  5:17-18 53
  5:18 60
  5:27-28 60
  5:41 49
  5:45 210
  5:48 202
  6:12 148

6:14-15 .... 148, 149
6:24 15
7:3 129
7:13 24
11:28-30 215
12:28 101
12:30 101
12:31-32 100
12:33 101
18:21-22 118
18:23-33 133
19:21 203
20:1-16 130
22:37-40 52
23:13, 15 .... 55, 99
23:23-24 60
25:31-46 26

Mark
2:27 43
10:21 203
12:29 196

Luke
1:33 157
5:32 72
7:41-42 117
7:46 117
11:11-13 87
15:11-32 .... 88, 201

John
3:17 150
8:11 49
8:12 16
8:36 152
14:6 28
20:23 149

Acts
3:19 85
10:15-16 10

17:27-28 4

Romans
1:17 25
2:24 193
2:25-27 45
2:29 46
3:10-12 212
3:23-24, 26 213
3:25-26 108
4:5 214
5:6-8 126
5:6-11 72
5:10 156
6:2-4 136
6:6-7 76
6:9-10 104
6:14 79
7:5-6 .... 77, 178
7:5, 10-11 36
7:6 .... 51, 79
7:7 39
7:12 51
7:14 179
7:18-20 .... 7, 76, 176
7:19 78
7:20 179
7:24 179
7:25 .... 77, 177, 179
8:1 179
8:1-2 36
8:4, 8-9 178
8:9 180
8:35-39 82
8:38 .... 168, 171
9:14-16 130
13:9-10 52

1 Corinthians
2:2 147

6:9-10	65
6:11	185
9:27	173
10:14-33	47
15:29	85

2 Corinthians

5:17-19	88
6:2	151
6:14	166

Galatians

2:21	183
3:19	39
3:24	39
4:9	170
5:2	45
5:2-12	194
5:4	170
5:18	44
6:15	45, 46

Ephesians

2:1-5	73
2:8-9	25
2:10	27
3:18-20	152
4:22-24	121
4:23-24	148
5:1-2	64
5:8-9	16

Philippians

3:8-10	146

Colossians

1:12-14	128
1:21-23	68
1:22	145
1:22-23	10
2:13-14	159
2:13-15	86
3:5	162

3:9-10	74

1 Timothy

1:8-11	50
1:13	120, 198
1:15-16	195, 197, 198
2:13	196

1 Thessalonians

2:12	200
4:12	200

2 Thessalonians

1:5, 11	200

Hebrews

3:5-6	157
4:15	10
7:25	110
8-9	158
8:12	85
9:14	10
9:15	109
9:26	104
9:26-28	159
10:2	104
10:10	104
10:12	104
10:14	104, 135, 204
10:18	105
10:23-31	68
10:26	121
12:18-24	146

James

1:14-15	61, 65
2:8-11	41
2:9	39
2:17-18	26
4:4-8	160
4:8	116
4:17	95

1 Peter

1:19	10
2:22	10
3:18	104
4:8	55
5:8	7

2 Peter

1:3-4	20
1:5-8	21
1:9	21
2:20-22	68

1 John

1:5	16
1:7	85, 111
1:8, 10	185
1:9	185
2:1-2	81
2:18	98
3:4	59, 165
3:5	11, 166
3:6,9	10
3:7-8	210
4:10	154
4:16	163
4:17-18	136
4:18	137
4:19	56
5:16-17	62, 65, 205, 207
5:18	62, 208

Revelation

22:17	140

Made in the USA
Las Vegas, NV
04 May 2023

71566011R00134